A HISTORY OF THE GUILLOTINE

The modern guillotine

A HISTORY OF
THE GUILLOTINE

ALISTER KERSHAW

Il faut avouer que les inventeurs des arts mécaniques ont été bien plus utiles aux hommes que les inventeurs des syllogismes.

VOLTAIRE

BARNES
&NOBLE
BOOKS
NEW YORK

This edition published by Barnes & Noble, Inc.

1993 Barnes & Noble Books

ISBN 1-56619-153-X

Printed and bound in the United States of America

M 9 8 7 6 5 4 3 2 1

CONTENTS

ILLUSTRATIONS

INTRODUCTION

W HEN even an occasional Frenchman expresses surprise on learning that the guillotine is still used to dispose of his homicidal compatriots, clearly it is time to add to the rich catalogue of books dealing exclusively or in part with that remarkable implement. To revive an appreciation of the high motives which lay behind its creation, to help distinguish between fact and fantasy in its history, to add a few hitherto unknown details, to give some account of the unconsidered officials who operate it: such is the aim of and the excuse for the present work.

★

Despite this lamentable ignorance that good Dr Guillotin's theories continue to be given practical application, I have assumed from the beginning that no one is without a reasonably accurate idea of the appearance of the guillotine. If even this should be too optimistic an assumption, all such dunces should glance at the frontispiece before going further.

On the other hand, English readers may be forgiven if they are unacquainted with a few words which occur in the text and which, since they could only be translated by the use of inconvenient phrases, I have left in French. The "bascule" for example, is the movable platform on which the condemned man is laid. Hinged, it stands vertically in the initial stages of an execution; the victim is pushed violently against it, whereupon it—and he—fall parallel with the ground, the man being thus face-downward with his neck between the uprights.

His throat is then resting in a semicircular depression cut in the lower of two planks set edgewise between the uprights; the upper plank (which may be shifted up and down) is swiftly lowered onto the nape of his neck, completing the circle and holding his head in position. This is the "lunette", in appearance and principle roughly resembling the stocks.

The blade of the guillotine is set into an eighty-pound metal weight known as the "mouton" and is hauled to the top of the frame by a rope. It is the "mouton's" four wheels, a pair on each side, one above the other, which run in the metal-lined grooves on the inner sides of the uprights. The "mouton" is surmounted by a spike in the shape of an arrow-head; this is forced into a sprung grab set in the top cross-bar which holds the whole thing in readiness; when the moment arrives, the executioner presses a lever—the "déclic"—which separates the jaws of the grab and so releases the ponderous mass for its downward journey.

Finally, I have found it convenient from time to time to employ the word "bourreau" in speaking of the headsman. It is an injurious term, much resented by the functionary to whom it has for so long been applied; but it is used of him more often than any other and, except to his too-sensitive ears, does not necessarily any longer imply disgust or revulsion. I have also sometimes referred to him as "Monsieur de Paris", a traditional title the origin of which is discussed later in this study.

*

After much more thought, no doubt, than the problem was worth, I decided to provide footnotes to show where each piece of information came from. These are disagreeable things; but if not included, an undeserved impression of plagiarism is given to those who know the sources, of omniscience to those who don't. As will be seen, some of the works quoted are necessarily obscure; but, wherever possible, I have given preference to popular works (so long as they were completely accurate) over the more specialised ones. I have also tried to avoid citing works which would seem portentously out of place in this modest history, quoting Lenotre rather than Cochin and Madelin rather than Sorel.

In quoting from documents on file in the various archives, I have, whenever the document in question has already appeared in some book or other, given that book as reference on the assumption that it would be more accessible to most readers wanting further details than the official dossier would be.

For all books mentioned I have referred to whatever edition I happened myself to read—hence, not necessarily to the first edition.

★

This history of the guillotine was originally to have been written in collaboration with my friend M. Jacques Delarue of the "Sûreté Nationale". It soon became clear, however, that we envisaged it quite differently, his interest being primarily in the sociology and psychology of the executioners, mine in the physical history of the machine and, to some extent, the intellectual and emotional atmosphere surrounding its proposal and adoption.

As a result, we decided that each should write his own book, which would be in part complementary and, of course, in part identical; meanwhile we would continue to share the results of our researches. This plan has been duly followed; M. Delarue is at least as much responsible as myself for whatever is of interest in the present work; and his own book (to be published in French) will incorporate much material which did not fit into the scheme of this one.

My thanks are due to a number of others; particularly to Miss Alannah Coleman and Mme Pamela Davies. Mr Noel Sharp of the British Museum Reading Room was always patient and helpful in the face of wearisomely frequent requests for information; Mr Richard Aldington, Mr and Mrs David Bartlett, Mr Robert Carter, M. Jean Chevalier, Mr and Mrs Geoffrey Dutton and Mr Charles Jordan all helped me in various ways.

I am greatly indebted to the distinguished historian, M. Pierre D'Espezel, for making available to M. Delarue and myself the remarkable manuscript by Dr Louis' descendant, Emile Begin, which forms the basis of Chapter Five, and for a number of other unpublished documents. M. F. Le Bour'his-Kerbiziet most courteously advised me on the history of the guillotine and the executioners in Brittany.

Finally, my thanks are due to the staff of the Archives Nationales; to the Keeper of the Edinburgh Museum of Antiquities for information on the Maiden and for permission to reproduce a photograph of that implement; to the Director of the Halifax Museums for details concerning the Halifax Gibbet; and to Madame Tussaud's Ltd for some facts in connection with the guillotine blade in their possession.

CHAPTER ONE

THE GUILLOTINE: from the day of its birth, and before then, this fantastical scarecrow loomed hugely in men's imaginations, established itself with a weird and unforeseeable persistence in their minds. Its manufacture was proposed, and forthwith it became a theme for popular songs and journalistic wit; it was built, and at once was reproduced in miniature as a decoration for the drawing-room or as a brooch or as earrings; it emerged as the hero of novels and pantomimes, was sketched and caricatured like an Elder Statesman, it was used as a motif for designs on snuff-boxes and cups and plates. During the Revolution, aristocratic ladies would set up a small model guillotine on the dinner table; tiny effigies of Fouquier or Robespierre would be placed between the uprights; the blade falls—from the doll's severed neck, a jet of scarlet; the ladies dip their handkerchiefs in the liquid. It is an elegant perfume.[1]

And what an incomparable toy for the children! In September of 1794, the *Conseil général* of Arras discovered that the infants of the district were diverting themselves by lopping off the heads of mice and birds with the aid of little guillotines two feet high. Robespierre had just fallen and ferocity was no longer fashionable; the Council ordered the police to seize these playthings which "although only intended as an amusement might imbue (the children) with notions of death and

---

[1] See Edmond and Jules de Goncourt: *Histoire de la société française pendant la Révolution* (Flammarion-Fasquelle, Paris, no date).

hence extinguish all humanitarian feeling". The confiscation was carried out; fur and feathers were found cemented to the toys with blood.[1]

The guillotine: it was more, much more than a toy; it was the symbol of a religion, it was an altar-piece, it was the altar itself, and Amar summoned his fellow deputies to join him there "to see the red Mass celebrated".[2] When, on June 8th, 1794, Robespierre conducted his service in praise of the Supreme Being, the guillotine was draped in blue velvet embroidered with roses and given its place in the quasi-religious celebrations.[3]

The profusion of its pet names, too, is significant, as though the coiners were seeking through derision to diminish its menace. That term itself—the guillotine—was only gradually made official after a royalist periodical [4] first jokingly suggested it almost as soon as busy little Dr Guillotin got up to urge on the States-General the advantages of a simple head-chopping mechanism. Later, when Dr Louis presented detailed plans for its construction, *Louison* and *Louisette* had a brief vogue; under the Terror—sometimes, it is said, separating heads from bodies at the rate of nearly one a minute [5]—it became the People's Avenger, the National Razor, the Patriotic Shortener; alone exempted from the law of equality, it was Lady Guillotine, was—only half in jest—canonised as Saint Guillotine; while the anonymous makers of underworld argot contributed a lexicon of their own—*la Veuve, l'Abbaye de Monte-à-Regret*, the *butte*, the *bascule*. . . . The uneasy slang has even made provision for each individual part of the

---

[1] See A.-J. Paris: *La Terreur dans le Pas-de-Calais et dans le Nord: Histoire de Joseph Lebon et des tribunaux révolutionnaires d'Arras et de Cambrai* (Rousseau-Leroy, Arras, 1864).

[2] See Louis Madelin: *La Révolution* (Hachette, Paris, 1938).

[3] See Edmond Biré: *Autour de la Révolution* (Librairie Catholique Emmanuel Vitte, Paris-Lyon, 1912).

[4] See *Les Actes des Apôtres*, t. I (*Du Jour des Morts* 1789 *au Jour de la Purification*, 1790).

[5] See G. D. F. (Guyot de Fère): *Notice historique et physiologique sur le supplice de la guillotine* (Paris, 1830).

hallucinating machine: the upper part of the *lunette* is the "head-breaker", the weight which adds to the velocity of the blade is the "travelling bag", the extra-large wicker container used to receive the corpses at a double or triple execution is the "family picnic basket".

One way or another, the guillotine is a favourite feature of the tattoo marks with which the French criminal classes adorn themselves [1]—its employment in this regard having been perfected by the sardonic convict who had his neck encircled with a ring of tattooed dots, surmounted by the indelible instruction: Cut along the dotted line; and it was soon found to be invariably good for a laugh in parliamentary circles— Desmoulins, for instance, having much success with his reference to the executioner as "*le représentant du pouvoir exécutif*".[2]

For a long time it was a sort of theatrical prop which dominated even the star performers: its functioning was critically examined and commented on by the newspapers and to such an extent that an assistant executioner could observe after watching his master's début, "He did very well, but I'm afraid he'll get a bad press." [3] No mere wheel or gibbet or axe ever inspired so many nicknames, such an abundance of vivacious humour, so intense an interest; those primitive contraptions were looked on with indifference by all but a few delicate individuals shuddering with an untimely revulsion.

Not that the guillotine has escaped censure. It had been operating barely fifty years when Charles Dickens, on a visit to Rome where it was among the amenities introduced by Napoleon's troops, attended an execution near (of all places!) the church of San Giovanni decollàto. He had not a good word to say for the business; the scaffold was "an untidy, unpainted,

---

[1] See Jacques Delarue and Robert Giraud: *Les Tatouages du 'milieu'* (La Roulotte, Paris, 1950).

[2] See Madelin, op. cit.

[3] See Georges Grison: *Souvenirs de la place de la Roquette* (E. Dentu, Paris, 1883).

uncouth, crazy-looking thing" and the whole operation "an ugly, filthy, careless, sickening spectacle".[1]

There is nothing surprising about Dickens' distaste; one would not want to deny him the right to his opinion; but—and here is the oddity—the guillotine has also evoked a positively love-sick admiration.

"The day before I left Rome," one of Lord Byron's correspondents was informed, "I saw three robbers guillotined. The ceremony—including the *masqued* priests; the half-naked executioners; the bandaged criminals; the black Christ and his banner; the scaffold; the soldiery; the slow procession, and the quick rattle and heavy fall of the axe; the splash of the blood, and the ghastliness of the exposed heads—is altogether more impressive than the vulgar and ungentlemanly 'new drop', and dog-like agony of infliction upon the sufferers of the English sentence. . . ."[2]

But Byron and Dickens were the *nineteenth* century; the appreciation of the one and the revulsion of the other are equally unrelated to the guiding principles of the century before, when the guillotine was created. Then, it was not the *æsthetics* of the thing which mattered, but the *ethics*; and the new method of slaughtering was—who could fail to see it?—morally delightful, reflecting credit on the age which produced it.

There were one or two drawbacks, of course. Had not the *Procureur général syndic* been obliged within a year of the guillotine's inauguration to admonish a colleague that "there have been complaints that after public performances of criminal sentences, the victims' blood remains where it is spilt and dogs come to drink it . . ."? But such coarse features of the new technique were promptly dealt with, the *Procureur* merely instructing his associate to "take what measures you consider most suitable and speedy to ensure that henceforward

[1] See Charles Dickens: *Pictures from Italy* (Sheldon & Co., New York, 1865).

[2] See Lord Byron: *Letters* (Everyman's Library, London, 1936).

this spectacle, so painful for humanity, shall no longer affront men's eyes".[1]

The appeal to humanitarian feelings is affecting; the more so since there is little question but that credit for the creation of the guillotine belongs precisely to humanitarians. Dr Guillotin certainly proposed it, Dr Louis certainly designed it, the German piano-maker, Tobias Schmidt, certainly built it; but its origin was with none of these. The guillotine has a vastly more distinguished parentage: Montesquieu, Rousseau, Voltaire, the *Encyclopédistes*, no less—these were the true begetters of the *machine à décoller*.

We tend, absurdly, to think of any given epoch in terms of its intellectuals, genuinely believing, for instance, that Descartes was more influential in his time than, say, the Duke of Marlborough in his. Pathetic delusion! But those who wish can find solace in remembering that the eighteenth century at least really was what other centuries never were—to a large extent, the product of its philosophers. Bliss was it in that dawn to be alive when the exquisite subversion of the *salons* really had some effect.

Self-important Dr Guillotin, the newly-elected deputy eager to have his say on any topic which might come up, was scarcely an intellectual: he was a politician: but his immortal recommendations to the Assembly happened to be made in 1789, and no one among the politicians at that moment (if he knew anything about his job) could possibly pronounce on any subject without toeing the line laid down by intellectuals in the course of the preceding hundred years.

"The common and unthinking assumptions of most ordinary men and women in the seventeenth century", one authority asserts, included the belief that "legal and social inequality, feudal privilege and arbitrary government were part of the permanent order of things and unalterable. By 1789 these instinctive assumptions had been replaced by another

---

[1] See Jules Taschereau: *Revue Retrospective*, t. l, 2e série, 1835.

system of ideas in the minds of almost all the urban population of France, and its social . . . aspects were accepted with equal enthusiasm by the peasantry." [1]

It is possible to suspect that the life of the French proletariat in the eighteenth century may not have been exactly as portrayed in *A Tale of Two Cities*. Feudal dues, as a matter of sobering fact, amounted to about two per cent of the gross product of the soil, and when, in 1790, the Church land was sold, the peasantry was able to invest billions of francs in its purchase.[2] A fascinating compilation has already been made from the attestations of astonished foreigners who visited pre-Revolutionary France in happy expectation of a chance to deplore the notorious poverty and misery of the country. Everywhere they encountered a people well fed, well dressed, strong, healthy and, above all, gay. Could there be some truth in the suggestion that one of the causes of the French Revolution was that "France, in the time of Louis XVI, was too happy"? [3]

Few people would now claim that the speculative lawyers who emerged from the provinces to join the States-General were wholly benign in their influence, and one cannot help but be struck by the fact that of the 2,567 women whom they executed in their libertarian enthusiasm, 1,447 belonged to the lower classes.[4] In 1789, however, the benefits of a New Order could not be foreseen; the thinkers had propagandised effectively; and that remarkable compost of Voltairean *realpolitik*, Rousseau's tipsy Moral Rearmament, and the eager reformism of the *Encyclopédistes* had not only gained the approval of the public but "had become a religion to the deputies who met in the States-General".[5]

[1] See Kingsley Martin: *French Liberal Thought in the Eighteenth Century* (Turnstile Press Ltd), London, 1954.

[2] See Ernest F. Henderson: *Symbol and Satire in the French Revolution* (G. P. Putnam's Sons, New York, 1912).

[3] See Georges Lenotre: *La Vie à Paris pendant la Révolution* (Calmann-Levy, Paris, 1936).

[4] See Biré, op. cit.

[5] See Kingsley Martin, op. cit.

A penal system which provided for protracted and inventive executions (and very often to punish crimes which the philosophers held to be no crimes at all but virtues born of their own teaching) was clearly bound to attract the reformers' attention. Less than thirty years before, Jean Calas had been broken on the wheel because of a rumour that he had killed his son to prevent the latter's conversion to Catholicism; and Voltaire had had a thing or two to say about it. And eight years before that, Damiens had been led out, unrecognisable after two months' torture in the Conciergerie, so that his life might be publicly ended at last. The hand which had struck so ineffectually at Louis XV was burnt away; molten lead and boiling oil were poured into his wounds. Four horses were set to dragging him apart, and when their strength proved inadequate—after sufficient time had been given them—the executioner used his knife to loosen the victim's joints a little and permit the horses to do their work before it grew too dark for the audience to see.[1]

The business was horribly out of keeping with eighteenth-century feeling; and besides, after blaming first the Jesuits and then the Jansenists for Damiens' mischievousness, the Government had tried to hold the *philosophes* themselves responsible. Reform of the penal code became a matter of immediate personal concern to the philosophers.

Louis XVI had abolished the tortures—the "question"—which had hitherto, as in Damiens' case, preceded the actual execution; but there remained on the statutes a prettily-graded range of *forms* which the executions might take. Fire awaited all magicians, sorcerers and heretics; the wheel was ready for highwaymen and assassins; lèse-majesté led to quartering; the vulgar who committed any of the 115 capital offences were hanged, the gentry decapitated.[2]

[1] See Jean Graven: *Le Problème de la peine de mort* (*Revue de Criminologie et de la Police technique*, janvier-mars, 1952).
[2] See A. Lacassagne: *Peine de mort et criminalité* (A. Maloine, Paris, 1908),

Beccaria had come out for the total abolition of the death penalty on the ground that it was grotesque to employ public murder in an effort to discourage private murder; Voltaire had enthusiastically taken up the notion, with implacable common sense suggesting that criminals should be obliged to work for the benefit of society—"their deaths offer no advantage except to the executioner"; Diderot (who had calculated the annual average of executions at three hundred—bad enough, but in a nation of eighteen million not quite as paralysing as the pro-Revolutionaries have hinted) joined in with a more quali-fied approval. But what irked their modest disciple, Dr Guillotin—child of his enlightened epoch, but not too much so—was less the business of putting to death than the lament-able differentiation in the means. Sword for one class, rope for another: the discrimination was insulting.

Not that he was wholly indifferent to the question of human suffering and its alleviation: neither he nor his fellow legislators could afford to be. The time was some little way off when intellectual gentility would be typified by the Abbé Morellet's recommendation that a "national butcher's shop" be estab-lished "according to the plans of the great artist and patriot David", that a law should be introduced requiring citizens to make a purchase there at least once a week on pain of imprison-ment or worse, and that its goods should be served "at every patriotic festival", progressively becoming "the true Com-munion of patriots, the Jacobins' Eucharist". The stock of this establishment was to consist of the flesh of victims of the guillotine.[1]

Proposals for such gastro-intellectual treats would have been hopelessly unsuited to the Assembly of 1789 where Robes-pierre himself grew tearful at the thought of man destroying man, even to uphold the law. Liberty, equality, fraternity per-sonified by Academicians chewing up dukes and marchionesses

[1] See Jacques Castelnau: *Le Comité de Salut Publique* (Librairie Hachette, Paris, 1941).

—it was inadmissible. And there was a fourth goddess who would have been as much dismayed by the suggestion: Reason itself would have protested. That was important. The philosophers who exercised so powerful an influence on their contemporaries had themselves been influenced, and most profoundly, perhaps, by the seventeenth-century scientists. Voltaire proclaimed a passion for Newtonian physics, numbers of his brother-philosophers had actually written books of a scientific character: rationality was as sacred as liberty, as equality, as fraternity.

Then how beautifully harmonious were the submissions of Dr Guillotin! They met every requirement of the age. An end to those snobbish executions—that took care of equality and fraternity, permitting a brotherly sharing of the same scaffold; head-chopping might be somewhat inconsistent with absolute liberty, but at least it restricted freedom as painlessly as possible; as to rationality—could anything be more rational than the brisk little gadget Dr Guillotin had in mind? The guillotine was philosophy made concrete.

CHAPTER TWO

"BY what strange stroke of fate did a man such as this, devoid of either talent or repute, bequeath that fearful immortality to his name?"[1] Dr Guillotin's admiring family, while disputing the judgement, would have been happy to furnish an explanation. According to a cherished tradition, his birth was accompanied by an augury almost unbearably apropos and which made that immortality inevitable. His mother, the story goes,[2] in the last stages of pregnancy but still able to take her promenade, came unexpectedly on the spectacle of a criminal undergoing the torture of the Wheel. It was only 1738, hardly yet the time for such displays of sensibility, but Mme Guillotin was so stricken as to be precipitately brought to bed. Joseph-Ignace Guillotin was born at Saintes the next day, May 28th. Those with a taste for pre-natal influences can scarcely avoid drawing the moral.

Environmentalists, on the other hand, will attribute that humanitarianism and revulsion from human suffering which are conventionally ascribed to Guillotin rather to his domestic and social background. His father was a provincial lawyer; if he was anything like his younger colleagues he was surrounded by the productions of contemporary thinkers and especially those dealing with judicial problems. It is easy to imagine the

[1] See François Bonneville: *Portraits de personnages célèbres de la Révolution, avec tableau historique et notices par P. Quenard* (Imprimerie du Cercle social, Paris, 1796–1802).

[2] See Pierre Quentin-Bauchart: *Le Docteur Guillotin et la guillotine* (Edition de la Nouvelle Revue, Paris, 1905).

youthful Guillotin precociously brooding over his parent's copy of Montesquieu's *Esprit des Lois*, let us say, and thereby conditioning his future career.

He was the product of a Jesuit upbringing, had even received the four minor orders from the hands of Mgr the Archbishop of Bordeaux himself; more specific than the environmentalists, the pious (if they can forget the Church's liking about that time for torturing heretics to death) will contend that this ghostly counsel produced a thoroughgoing Christian with all a Christian's determination to succour the distressed.

Finally, there are those believers in the *zeitgeist* who will insist that, given no matter what prodigious symbolism about the child-bed or what lack of it, given no matter what heredity, upbringing or education, anyone born in that century of enlightenment was bound to take on the splendid lineaments of the humanitarian.

Documentation on Guillotin's life is so deplorably sparse that it is impossible to prove or disprove any of the theories. All that one can say is that, for a dedicated lover of mankind, the Doctor waited a long time before getting to work. True, having decided to let his novitiate's tonsure grow over, he took up the practice of medicine, but even that does not necessarily demonstrate the existence of a passion for the human race; and the fact remains that he was nearly fifty before he entered that political world which humanitarians ordinarily enter at the earliest possible age.

Prior to 1788 the Doctor evinced no sign of political awareness, benefiting humanity—if that was what he was about—only by occupying the post of *docteur-régent* at the Paris Faculty of Medicine, by functioning as professor of anatomy, physiology and pathology, and by sitting on the Royal Commission appointed to investigate the disquieting theories propounded by M. Mesmer.

That last is perhaps significant. Royal Commissions are customarily made up of individuals with a nascent or flourishing resolution to contribute to the general good. Was it his experience of setting the world right on mesmerism which first led Dr Guillotin to think that his views should be made available on still graver topics to a still wider public?

However that may be, in 1788 he published his *Pétition des Citoyens domiciliés à Paris*, claiming a representation for the Third Estate in the new Assembly equal to that of the nobles and the ecclesiastics together. The suggestion was scandalous and adroit; things worked out wonderfully; public opinion was aroused; the Doctor was summoned to explain himself before Parliament; his pamphlet was suppressed, just as if it had been some subversive work by Voltaire; his political career was made. In the following year, the pamphleteering medico became a deputy representing that Third Estate which he had so stoutly bespoken and which he so admirably typified.

And then what a time! What earnest activity, what conscientious application, what opportunities for handing out gratuitous advice! "Judicious Guillotin", as Carlyle affectionately calls him, "can improve the ventilation of the hall; in all cases of medical police and *hygiène* be a present aid"; he can even dredge up an opinion—and pass it on to the President of the Assembly—concerning the arrangement of the carpet when the King is to make a visit to that body.[1] Judicious Guillotin, indeed; or, if one prefers it, "an insignificant man, but meddlesome, with a finger in every pie—a busybody, in fact".[2]

Carpets and ventilation are all very well for a time, but they cannot satisfy the public-spiritedness of a man like Guillotin for ever. When, on October 9th, 1789, a debate on the Penal Code opened in the Assembly, he must have felt that here was an occasion worthier of a man who had been asked to give his opinions on mesmerism, who had had a pamphlet suppressed,

[1] See Thomas Carlyle: *The French Revolution* (Macmillan & Co., London, 1900).
[2] See Bonneville, op. cit.

whose signature on legislative documents appeared side by side with those of the baron de Marguerittes, the marquis de Bonnay, the comte de Castellane, who was on familiar terms with such other members of the *Club de 1789* as Saint-Etienne, Kersaint and André Chénier.[1] On the second day of the debate, Dr Guillotin submitted a proposition in six articles which included a recommendation that death, without the accompaniment of torture and by means of decapitation, should become the sole and standard form of capital punishment. His discourse was received with exuberant applause and some members were so overcome that they actually urged the unprecedented course of dealing with the question immediately.[2] In the end, however, the orthodox routine of all legislative bodies was followed and the Assembly voted that any consideration of the matter be decently adjourned.

One hesitates to accept the jeering allegation[3] that the Doctor simply "thought it expedient to prepare for himself a good reception from his constituents" by so forthrightly associating himself with plans to ameliorate a sentence which (they were uneasy times) might one day be visited on any of them. The suggestion, in fact, reveals an unawareness of the psychology of such men as Guillotin: their scurryings are never for reasons of expediency; they busy themselves because it is their pleasure to do so—genuinely *ars gratia artis*.

His admirers, of course, insist on the splendid disinterestedness of the great scheme, but it is a pity that none of them has produced any evidence that the Doctor was motivated by a concern with suffering mankind. Even the indefatigable persistence with which he ensured that his propositions were not pigeon-holed might as easily be taken to demonstrate a regard for his private dignity as for that of his fellow creatures, but,

[1] See Hector Fleischmann: *La Guillotine en 1793* (Librairie des Publications modernes, Paris, 1908).
[2] See *Le Moniteur*, October 11th, 1789.
[3] See John Wilson Croker: *History of the Guillotine* (John Murray, London, 1853).

whatever his motives, on December 1st, 1789, up he popped to present his six articles for the second time:[1]

"1. Offences of the same kind will be punished by the same kind of penalty whatsoever the rank and station of the guilty parties.

"2. In all cases where the law imposes the death penalty on an accused person, the punishment shall be the same, whatever the nature of the offence of which he is guilty; the criminal shall be decapitated; this will be done solely by means of a simple mechanism.

"3. In view of the personal character of crime, no punishment of a guilty person shall involve any discredit to his family. The honour of those belonging to him shall be in no way soiled, and they shall continue to be no less admissible to any kind of profession, employment and public function.

"4. No one shall reproach a citizen with any punishment imposed on one of his relatives. Whosoever ventures to do so shall be publicly reprimanded by the judge. The sentence imposed on him shall be written up on the offender's door. Moreover, it shall be written up on the pillory and remain there for a period of three months.

"5. Confiscation of the condemned person's property shall in no case be imposed.

"6. The corpse of an executed man shall be handed over to his family on their request. In every case, he shall be allowed normal burial and no reference shall be made on the register to the nature of his death."

No proposals could have been more exactly calculated to gratify the prevailing public mood. And what a piece of real genius, what a *coup de maître* was Article 4, compensating for the suppression of old crimes by creating a new one! Dr Guillotin's political acumen was never more apparent.

If only one could read his address! But it has tragically vanished, was not even among the papers bequeathed to his

[1] See *Journal des Débats et des Décrets*, December 1st, 1789.

heirs, and the following[1] is as comprehensive an account of the memorable occasion as exists:

"Drawing a picture as vivid as it was sensitive of the ghastly tortures which have persisted even up to the present humanitarian century—the gibbets, the wheels, the scaffolds, the stakes; barbarous tortures conceived by a barbarous feudal system, he concluded that there should be only one punishment of the same kind for all crimes.[2] Here M. Guillotin dwelt on the tortures which place mankind lower than the wild beasts: the use of pincers, etc. I pass over them", observes the reporter primly, "in silence."

All very proper, of course; but, unhappily, the fellow also chooses to pass over in silence the meat (so to speak) of the Doctor's speech, noting merely that "M. Guillotin described the mechanism (of his proposed beheading device), the effect of which he pictured—momentarily abandoning the role of legislator for that of orator—by saying: the mechanism falls like thunder; the head flies off; blood spurts; the man is no more".

The too sensitive reporter has thus deprived us for ever of any definite knowledge as to how far Dr Guillotin had elaborated his plans. Inferentially, as will be seen, it can be assumed that he did no more than throw out some rudimentary ideas on the construction of a head-chopping machine; and, in any case, however detailed they may have been, his plans, as will also be seen, were supplanted by others; but the teasing possibility remains that perhaps Dr Guillotin really did submit a precise project for a machine which was never built. One would give much to know.

Press reaction to the Doctor's speech was enthusiastic, the newspapers applauding "the humane sentiments which breathed

---

[1] See *Journal des Etats généraux*, December 1st, 1789.

[2] The suggestion that one specific punishment was to be handed out for all crimes from petty larceny to high treason is lavishly misleading. What Guillotin actually proposed, of course, was that there should be only one punishment for *each* crime, without regard to the social standing of the condemned person.

in the Guillotin proposals"[1] and the "great principles of criminal jurisprudence"[2] embodied there. One commentator[3] revealed that not only the criminal but the executioner as well benefited from Guillotin's ingenuity, remarking that "the innovation of replacing the executioner with a mechanism which, like the law itself, separates the sentence from the judge, is worthy . . . of the new order into which we are about to enter".

The legislature, perhaps regretting its earlier unparliamentary emotion, was less carried away; all that that massive body could bring itself to do was to vote the first article of the six submitted, and Guillotin's own energy seems not to have survived that second disappointment. At all events, on January 21st, 1790, it was the Abbé Papin who recalled the Assembly's wandering attention to the business and Guillotin apparently contributed nothing towards obtaining approval, eventually given during this debate, of three more of his articles. These did not include the showpiece, the second article of his original Bill providing for decapitation by a machine, and, as a matter of fact, that particular article was never debated at all.[4]

This slighting treatment of his scheme must have been exceedingly galling to one with such a rugged determination to help his fellow-men even if it killed them, and it accounts perhaps for Guillotin sitting in gloomy silence during the next debate on the death penalty, which took place—there was no hurry—in June 1791. The two *vedettes* on this occasion both argued passionately that the philosophic gods required the complete suppression of the death penalty, any sort of death penalty. One of these abolitionists was M. Duport-Dutertre, later, as Minister of Justice, among those most closely connected with introducing the decapitating machine. The other

---

[1] See *Le Journal de Paris*, December 2nd, 1789.
[2] See *La Gazette de Paris*, December 4th, 1789.
[3] See *Le Moniteur*, December 18th, 1789.
[4] See Dr Archille Chéreau: *Guillotin et la guillotine* (Aux bureaux de l'Union médicale, Paris, 1870).

was M. Robespierre. Both ended under the blade of the guillotine.

The legend among those who like their irony good and strong is that Dr Guillotin himself was likewise finished off by his own "invention", but in reality, when he died (of a carbuncle in the shoulder) at his home in the rue St Honoré, there was nothing mechanical about the occasion whatever. True, during the Terror, that exhausting determination of his to bestow his opinions on the rest of the world landed him briefly in prison; it is even said that only Robespierre's fall saved him from being strapped to the *bascule*. It may be so; in any case, what is really remarkable is that he was *not* guillotined: few of his colleagues in the Assembly had as much luck.

His biographers are insistent that he could scarcely have suffered more from his own little wrinkle if it *had* been the direct means of killing him. "His venerable countenance", one acquaintance has recorded,[1] "bore the marks of a profound grief and his completely white hair was witness to what he had suffered." Everyone must decide for himself whether the laceration to Guillotin's *amour-propre* is more heart-rending than the thought of the thousands who were slaughtered by the implement which he had recommended; for *amour-propre* it certainly was which was involved. It was the identification of his name with "the exploits of his terrible offspring" [2] which distressed him, although it is hard to see why he should have wanted to spurn the credit for his own high-mindedness. But it was so; even though he managed to survive in the face of the embarrassment until the age of seventy-six, he abandoned his political career and became once more, in Carlyle's words,[3] the "respectable practitioner" but "doomed by a satiric destiny" to a grisly, partly unmerited immortality.

On June 3rd, 1791, the Assembly approved a text providing

[1] See Anonymous (Mlle Georgette Ducrest): *Mémoires sur l'impératrice Joséphine, la Cour et les Salons de Paris sous l'Empire* (Ladvocat, Paris, 1828).
[2] See Quentin-Bauchart, op. cit.
[3] See Carlyle, op. cit.

that "Every person condemned to the death penalty shall have his head severed". On September 25th of the same year, this decision was officially embodied in the new Penal Code. Not until March 20th, 1792, and after a ludicrous bureaucratic hullabaloo, was a decree forthcoming which laid down that such decapitation should be carried out by means of a machine, striking wrongdoers competently, impartially, and (as far as possible) kindlily, in the triple tradition of rationality, egalitarianism and humanitarianism.

An Irish "guillotine"

"The Diele"

"The Mannaia"

PLATE I

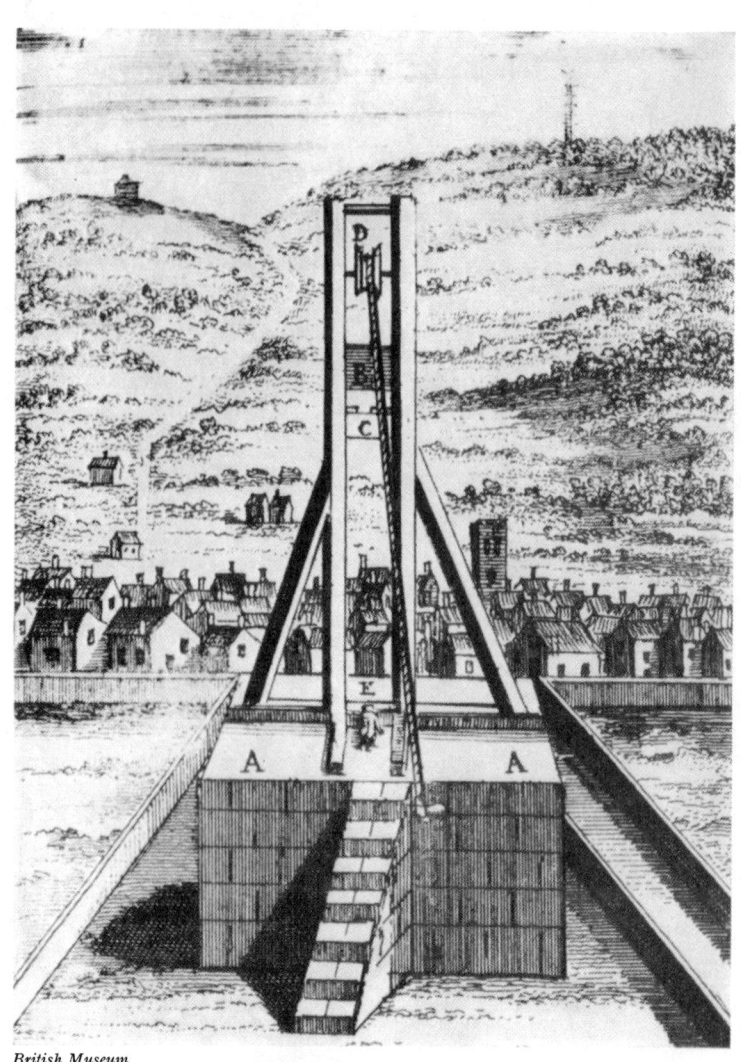

"The Halifax Gibbet"

PLATE II

CHAPTER THREE

D<small>R</small> G<small>UILLOTIN</small>'s part in creating the machine named after him has been variously appraised. Popularly, of course, he is regarded as its unique inventor and designer; one or two "authorities" on the subject are hardly less generous in estimating his importance; others deny that he contributed anything at all. Just how much of the Doctor's cheerless celebrity is deserved has already been discussed; here it is enough to recall that he did undoubtedly provide the Assembly, however sketchily, with some sort of plan for a decapitating machine, and it is probable that he envisaged something substantially the same as what was eventually built.

But it is equally certain that Guillotin *invented* nothing; he had no need to: the only problem confronting the earnest student—and it is an insoluble one—is to know which of the various prototypes inspired him. One writer [1] asserts that he first conceived his project while contemplating some bridge-builders using a pile-driver; another [2] that the notion came to him during a performance of the pantomime *Les Quatres Fils d'Aymon* in which some such gadget figured among the props. It is scarcely necessary to consider the triumphant claim [3] that the blade of a veritable Stone Age "guillotine" was unearthed

[1] See Maxime Du Camp: *Paris—ses organes, ses fonctions et sa vie dans la seconde moitié du XIXe siècle* (Hachette, Paris, 1869–75).

[2] See Edmond-Jean Guerin: *Le Docteur Guillotin* (N. Texier et fils, La Rochelle, 1908).

[3] See Georges Lenotre: *La guillotine et les exécuteurs des arrêts criminels pendant la Révolution* (Perrin et Cie, Paris, 1918).

in the Aisne in 1865, and the legend of Chinese and Persian machines can probably be written off as merely another contribution to the tradition that everything existed in the mystic East well before the pedestrian Occidentals thought of it. Achille Bocchi's *Symbolicarum quaestionum libri* has been cited [1] in support of the theory that the Spartans did their bit towards helping mechanical beheading along, and a local patriot [2] disinterred a work by the sixteenth-century Flemish poet, Joseph Cats, which gives a description of a decapitating mechanism, leaving one free to decide for oneself whether or not Dr Guillotin was a Cats reader.

Setting aside these picturesque fancies, it is assuredly a fact that France itself had developed a contrivance of the sort at least as early as the first half of the seventeenth century. A work published some fifty years after the event [3] provides an account of the Maréchal de Montmorency's execution at Toulouse in 1632 is of capital importance to this enquiry:

"A rope was thrown over his arm and he went to the scaffold, which he reached by a window, for in that country they use an axe (*une doloire*) which is between two pieces of wood, and when the head is placed on the block, the rope is released and the axe falls and separates the head from the body."

All honour to the Toulousians for having anticipated Guillotin, but despite their early appearance on the scene they cannot claim priority in the matter. Of the countries known to have employed the same address in getting rid of their unwanted citizens, it is Ireland (as far as can be verified) which first bestowed on mankind the art of mechanised head-chopping. The writer of an article on the guillotine [4] affirms that

---

[1] See Chéreau, op. cit.

[2] See l'Abbé Adolphe Bloeme: *Notice sur la guillotine* (Guermonprez, Hazebrouck, 1865).

[3] See *Les Mémoires de messire Jacques de Chastenet, chevalier, Seigneur de Puységur, colonel du régiment de Piedmont, sous les règnes de Louis XIII et de Louis XIV, etc., etc.* (J. Morel, Paris, 1690).

[4] See *The Popular Encyclopædia or Conversations Lexicon* (Blackie & Son, London & Glasgow, 1877).

five men were executed by the medium of a machine at Zittau in 1300, which, if true, would give Germany a seven-year lead over the Irish contenders, and that Conrad of Swabia was similarly dealt with at Naples in 1266, which would put Italy still further ahead; but the writer in question gives no authority for his revelations and the claim must be disallowed for that reason.

In Holinshed's *Chronicles*,[1] however, there is no such equivocation; there is the woodcut of an unmistakable "guillotine" (see Plate I) and the accompanying text proclaims flatly that it was used for the execution "near to Merton" of Murcod Ballagh on April 1st, 1307. No earlier mechanical removal of heads is recounted with details as precise, although the English, of course, have tried to filch this Irish distinction. One reads [2] that their Halifax Gibbet was in operation during the reign of Edward III, which still leaves old Ireland ahead; but the assertion has also been made that the Halifax implement was introduced into England by the Normans.[3] It may be so; and, in any case, one cannot go on endlessly assessing the justice of national pleas for recognition as the originators of this particular sport. What matters is that the Halifax Gibbet (and comparable machines elsewhere in Europe) unquestionably existed well before Guillotin's day and that reasonably precise descriptions of it have fortunately been preserved.

Once again it is Holinshed who instructs us:

"There is, and has been, of ancient time, a law or rather custom, at Halifax, that whosoever doth commit any felony, and is taken with the same, or confesses the fact upon examination, it be valued by four constables to amount to the sum of thirteenpence-halfpenny, he is forthwith beheaded upon one of the next market-days (which fall usually upon the Tuesdays,

---

[1] See Raphaell Holinshed: *Chronicles of England, Scotlande and Irelande* (John Harrison, London, 1577).

[2] See *The Penny Cyclopedia* (Charles Knight, London, 1833).

[3] See William Andrews: *Bygone Punishments* (Philip Allan & Co., London, 1931).

Thursdays, and Saturdays), or else upon the same day that he is convicted, if market be holden. The engine wherewith the execution is done is a square block of wood, of the length of four feet and a half, which doth ride up and down in a slot, rabet, or regall, between two pieces of timber that are framed and set upright, of five yards in height. In the nether end of a sliding block is an axe, keyed or fastened with an iron into the wood, which, being drawn up to the top of the frame, is there fastened by a wooden pin (with a notch made in the same, after the manner of a Samson's post), unto the middest of which pin is a long rope fastened, that cometh down among the people; so that when the offender hath made his confession, and hath laid his neck over the nethermost block, every man there present doth either take hold of the rope (or putteth forth his arm so near to the same as he can get, in token that he is willing to see justice executed), and pulling out the pin in this manner, the head-block wherein the axe is fastened doth fall down with such a violence, that if the neck of the transgressor were so big as that of a bull, it should be cut in sunder at a stroke. . . ."

Another writer [1] provides a few more details:

"If it was a horse, an ox, or any other creature, that was stol'n, it was brought along with him to the place of execution, and fasten'd to the cord by a pin that stay'd the block. So that when the time of execution came (which was known by the Jurors holding up one of their hands) the Bailiff or his Servant, whipping the beast, the pin was pluck'd out and execution done. But if it was not done by a beast, then the Bailiff or his Servant cut the rope."

There is apparently no way of knowing whether it was from the Halifax Gibbet that the Irish derived their machine, but the Scots are refreshingly candid in admitting that it was the

[1] See William Camden: *Britannia* (Edmund Gibson, London, 1722).

parent of their Maiden.[1] Describing the execution of the
Regent Morton in 1581, Sir Walter Scott reports [2] that "he
met his death with the same determined courage that he had
often displayed in battle; and it was remarked with interest by
the common people, that he suffered decapitation by a rude
guillotine of the period which he himself during his administration had introduced into Scotland from Halifax; it was
called the Maiden".

Unlike the Irish device, unlike the *doloire*, unlike the Halifax
Gibbet of which nothing remains but its stone emplacement,
or the guillotine itself which is hidden furtively away in a
gloomy hangar at the Santé prison, the Maiden has been preserved for public delectation and is installed at the National
Museum of Antiquities in Edinburgh. It has therefore been
possible to establish the appearance of this oddity with a precision not practicable in respect of any of its ancient counter-
parts:

"The Scottish machine is made of oak and consists of a sole
beam 5 feet in length into which are fixed two upright posts
10 feet in height, 4 inches broad and 12 inches apart from each
other, and $3\frac{1}{2}$ inches in thickness, with bevelled corners. These
posts are kept steady by a brace at each side which springs from
the end of the sole and is fastened to the uprights 4 feet from
the bottom. The tops of the posts are fixed into a cross rail
2 feet in length. The block is a transverse bar $3\frac{1}{4}$ feet from the
bottom, 8 inches in breadth and $4\frac{1}{2}$ inches in thickness, and a
hollow on the upper edge of this bar is filled with lead. . . .

"The axe consists of a plate of iron faced with steel; it
measures 13 inches in length and $10\frac{1}{2}$ inches in breadth. On

[1] Various origins for this name have been suggested. The popular (and
most entertaining) explanation is that the machine was so called because it
remained unused for a long time after its importation into Scotland. But
Charles Rogers in his *Social Life in Scotland* (William Paterson, Edinburgh,
1884–6) derives the word from the Celtic "mod-dun", meaning a place
where justice was administered.

[2] See Sir Walter Scott: *History of Scotland* (Longman, Rees, Orme, Brown,
Green and Taylor, London, 1830).

the upper edge of the plate was fixed a mass of lead 75 pounds
in weight. This blade works in grooves cut on the inner edges
of the uprights, which are lined with copper. . . ." [1]

The resemblance to the guillotine is striking, and, as if all
that were not enough, a manuscript description in the possession of the Society of Antiquities of Scotland even adds that
an archaic *lunette* was incorporated in the Maiden—a hinged
iron bar which was laid on the victim's neck so that he could
not draw back his head.

No such copious information is available regarding the
decapitating machines anciently used, we are told, in Germany.
"An instrument resembling the guillotine may be seen in the
old Nuremburg palace," says one writer,[2] "and if the guide
may be believed, it dates from two centuries ago." Was this
intriguing structure—destroyed now, of course—the *Diele* or
the *Hobel* or the *Dolabra*? All three names crop up in German
accounts of primitive Teutonic guillotines, but it is never
clear whether the names belong to one creation or to three.
Probably, three distinct machines are involved, since there are
basic variations in the workings as portrayed by various artists.
Some drawings, for example, show a blade which, like that of
the guillotine, was allowed to drop, and others a blade which
was laboriously forced through the neck with hammer blows.[3]
Or are all these representations fanciful?

Germany has always shown itself friendly to the principle of
head-chopping; it has a deserved reputation in the field; the
National Socialists' restoration of the uniformed headsman
and his ritualistic axe is a recent indication of the country's
taste; yet all references to Germanic crypto-guillotines are
vague and, if not implausible, undocumented. Were there no
memorialists, no letter-writers, no keepers of journals to note
the *diele* in action?

[1] See *Proceedings of the Society of Antiquities of Scotland*, Vol. III, 1886–8.
[2] See Fernand Nicolaÿ: *Curiosités historiques. Histoire sanglante de l'humanité.
La peine de mort: supplices capitaux chez tous les peuples* (P. Téqui, Paris, 1909).
[3] Communication from the Feldhaus-Archiv, Wilhelmshaven.

One is driven back to mere pictures—but pictures of what? On the face of it, the fact that German artists have portrayed a sort of mediæval guillotine might be considered proof that some such contraption existed in Germany in the Middle Ages. But the personages in these designs are almost invariably shown in Græco-Roman tunics and breastplates: for all one knows, the guillotines might be Græco-Roman, too.

There was a mural by Albrecht Dürer in the Nuremburg Town Hall which showed a *Diele*; but this was almost certainly introduced by a seventeenth-century restorer and, in any case, the whole lot was destroyed in the Second World War, which rather rules it out as evidence.[1] And a fifteenth-century mural in the Lorch chapel in Würtemburg shows the execution of Conrad of Swabia by similar means. The operation was carried out in Naples but the machine may have been German.[2]

But all this pictorial evidence is unconvincing. Those engravings by Pencz, Aldegrever and others, which are so often triumphantly adduced by the defenders of Germany's position in this business—what in fact is their value as evidence? The baron Adrien Wittert in his *Notices historiques sur les gravures de Jean de Bavière* [3] recounts that when, in the early fifteenth century, John of Bavaria quelled the revolt of the Liégeois democrats, he subjected the ringleaders to execution by a sort of guillotine. At least one contemporary artist was prompt to limn the scene; his design was copied by Lucas van Leyden; and it was this which was later copied in turn by Pencz and the others. We are left uncertain whether John of Bavaria found the instrument locally available or whether he brought it with him.

Almost one begins to doubt whether Germany ever made any contribution to mechanical decapitation, since forthright information in the manner of Camden and Holinshed is so

[1] Communication from the Germanisches National-Museum, Nuremburg.

[2] Communication from the Feldhaus-Archiv, Wilhelmshaven.

[3] Quoted by Georges de Froidcourt: *La Guillotine liégeoise et les exécuteurs des arrêts criminels* (Georges Thone, Liège, 1934).

conspicuously lacking. The most that one can do is to believe wistfully in the cumulative significance of different scraps of evidence, none of them persuasive in itself.

Happily, the Italian *mannaia* has been the subject of fuller treatment. An eighteenth-century traveller [1] has recorded that it consisted of "a framework four to five feet in height measuring about fifteen inches across between the inner surfaces. It is composed of two uprights measuring about three inches square and with grooves in them. . . . The two uprights are joined to each other by three cross-pieces fixed with tenons and mortices, one at each end and another fifteen inches above the one closing the bottom of the frame. It is on this last cross-piece that the victim places his head. Above this cross-piece is the movable cross-piece which slides in the grooves of the uprights. The lower part is furnished with a large sharp blade nine or ten inches long and six inches across. The upper part carries a weight of sixty to eighty pounds. This murderous cross-piece is raised to within an inch or two of the upper cross-piece, to which it is attached by a thin cord; when the captain of the guard signs to the executioner, he simply cuts this thin cord and the blade, falling directly on the victim's neck, cuts it cleanly."

Dr Guillotin was never so explicit, although the French perfectionists of 1792 would certainly have objected to Father Labat's assertion that the primitive object was "very sure and never keeps a subject waiting". It is not surprising to learn from the same writer that so expeditious and, as it would seem, almost agreeable a death was reserved for "gentlemen and ecclesiastics": it is only fitting. Indeed, we are informed that in England the luxury was not provided solely on the basis of social eligibility but was extended only "so long as the sufferers are ready to pay for it".[2]

[1] See Père Jean-Baptiste Labat: *Voyage d'Espagne et d'Italie* (J.-B. et C.-J.-B. Delespine, Paris, 1730.)

[2] No corroboratory evidence exists that the Halifax Gibbet—the only known English "guillotine"—was ever so commercialised.

There is an eye-witness account [1] of the *mannaia* at work as early as 1507, when, on May 13th, Demetrius Giustiniani (convicted of seditious activities) was led onto the scaffold, obliged to kneel and to place his head on the block. "*Le bourreau*" (it would be a pity to english the charming original) "*prinst une corde, a laquelle tenoit actaché ung groux bloc, a tout une douloere tranchant, hantée dedans, venant d'amont entre deux pousteaulx, et tire ladite corde, en maniere que le bloc tranchant a celui gennevoys tumba antre le teste et les espaules, si que le teste s'en va d'ung couste et le corps tumbe de l'autre.*"

There is, too, that bundle of Italian manuscripts edited by Stendhal [2] to support the belief that Beatrice Cenci and her family were executed by the *mannaia*. But the word "*mannaia*," after all, means no more than a "headsman's axe," whether mechanically operated or not, and we only have Stendhal's notation on the manuscript ("the *mannaia* resembled the French death instrument") to justify our thinking that it refers to anything more sophisticated on this occasion—that, and the original document's description of Beatrice "placing her head *under* the *mannaia*," which seems to hint at something other than an axe or a sword. Not that one can be sure: continental enthusiasts in this field are sometimes so carried away as to hold that Sir Thomas More was mechanically decapitated.

The fact is, however, that the more one investigates the question, the more the precursors of the guillotine seem to proliferate. Did the Dutch in Batavia in the early 1700's really use some such device on their slaves to encourage the others? [3] Is it true that the introduction of a comparable instrument into the Austro-Hungarian Empire in 1756 was only prevented by a lack of funds? [4] And what of poor, forgotten Councillor

---

[1] See Jean d'Auton: *Histoire de Louis XII* (A. Pacard, Paris, 1615).
[2] See Stendhal: *Les Cenci* (*Oeuvres de Stendhal*, Collection les Portiques, Paris, 1952).
[3] See J. W. Heydt: *Schau-Platz von Africa und Ost-Indien* (Willhermsdorff, 1744).
[4] See Graven, op. cit.

Meiner in Berlin, more than five years ahead of Guillotin in his concern with such good works? [1]

At all events, it is clear that no great inventive genius was called for on Dr Guillotin's part: he had only to pick and choose. There was no need for him to brood on the activities of pile-drivers or to experience any sudden flash of illumination while attending a pantomime. That lost description with which he favoured the Assembly must have been based on one or other of the foregoing contraptions, and it only remains to discover what were the novel touches which were brought to the French counterpart.

[1] See *Berlinische Monatsschrift*, May, 1785.

CHAPTER FOUR

TEN months, as already noted, were allowed to elapse between the Assembly's decision that all capital punishments should consist of decapitation and the issuance of a decree specifying the precise means to be employed. The romantic may choose to think that the authorities had begun to suspect the new law of being, after all, not quite so much in harmony with prevailing philanthropic sentiment as it had at first seemed; but it is likelier that this *entr'acte* was simply due to normal bureaucratic inertia. The delay may or may not have suited the condemned men awaiting a decision as to just how their forfeited heads were to be removed, but there was a horde of officials who felt that no criminal preferences compensated for the inconveniences to which they, the officials, were thus subjected. Murders were becoming increasingly frequent, prisons intolerably crowded, and in the very month when the Assembly adopted the fatal text, the brothers Agasse were hanged with bluff disregard for the new namby-pamby legislation.[1] Four months later, another fretful tribunal pointedly took note that there was still "no law specifying the means whereby a life is to be ended" and ordered that a certain Jacques Haas should be "hanged and strangled".[2]

Less wholeheartedly disobedient, the *commissaire du roi* at Falaise nonetheless in May of the following year (by which time an official machine had at last been built but not yet

[1] See Chéreau, op. cit.
[2] See Edmond Seligman: *La Justice en France pendant la Révolution* (Librairie Plon, Paris, 1901).

distributed to all departments) did have a pseudo-guillotine built to his own design and with it carried out the execution of one Duval Bertin.[1] Gratification with the results achieved by his little novelty was stronger than any remorse the *commissaire* may have felt over his insubordination and he sent the Minister of Justice an excited account of the "incalculable rapidity with which Duval Bertin's head was separated from his body. The speed", he wrote lyrically, "was that of the lightning-flash which announces and precedes the thunder. . . . Ten necks together could not resist the power produced by the speed of this instrument. . . ."

Other functionaries, as impatient if less adventurous, likewise troubled the massive immobility of their superiors during this long waiting period, and among the earliest of these gadflies was the great Charles-Henri Sanson himself, hereditary Executioner of the High Works. In a memorandum to the Minister of Justice, he pointed to some of the problems involved in the business of decapitation. In the old days, only an occasional nobleman enjoyed the privilege of losing his head, and *he* could be relied on to display a gentlemanly spirit of co-operation; but now, with all the riff-raff due to benefit from the same treatment. . . . Measuredly, Sanson let it be known that something more efficacious than the traditional sword was going to be needed:

"In order that the execution be completed according to the requirements of the law, it is necessary that, without any resistance on the part of the victim, the executioner should be very adroit, the condemned man very composed. Otherwise, it will never be possible to complete such an execution by the sword without the risk of dangerous incidents.

"After each execution, the sword is unfit for another; it is absolutely essential that the sword, which is liable to chip, should be sharpened and whetted anew if there are several condemned persons to be executed at the same time; it is

[1] See Seligman, op. cit.

therefore necessary to have a sufficient number of swords in a state of readiness. This opens the way to very great and almost insurmountable difficulties.

"It should further be noted that swords have often broken during such executions. . . .

"Consideration should be given to the possibility that, when several condemned persons are to be executed on the same occasion, the terror inspired by the execution—on account of the huge quantities of blood spread about—will cause fear and weakening in the most intrepid of those remaining to be executed. Such weaknesses will create a ruinous obstacle to the execution. . . . The execution will develop into a struggle and a massacre.

"It is therefore essential," Sanson concluded, "in order to satisfy the humanitarian opinions advanced by the National Assembly, that a means be found of immobilising the condemned man so that there can be no uncertainty in the execution. . . ." [1]

Views so weighted with authority could not be ignored; and an incongruous bustle began among the upper echelon of Paris officialdom. Letters and memoranda were henceforward exchanged at a furious pace between M. Roederer, the *Procureur général syndic*, M. Duport-Dutertre, the Minister of Justice (his expressed hostility to the death penalty in no way inhibiting him from assisting at the *accouchement* of that penalty's most effective aid), very infrequently Dr Guillotin himself, various judges and *commissaires du roi*, and a whole train of Finance Ministers. On March 3rd, 1792, with nothing practical achieved, despite all the bureaucratic flurry, the Administrators composing the *Directoire* of the Department of Paris put the problem squarely to the President of the National Assembly himself, informing him that:

"The Second Criminal Tribunal, obliged to have a death

[1] See Ludovic Pichon: *Code de la Guillotine* (Librairie générale de droit et de jurisprudence, Paris, 1910).

sentence carried out, has asked the *Directoire* of the Department how to apply Article 3 of the *Code Pénal* which provides as follows: Every person condemned (to the death penalty) shall have his head severed. The *Directoire* felt that, since the law did not stipulate the method of applying this article, it was not possible to specify any other than that employed in the past: but the executioner has voiced the fear that this would not meet the intention of the law: such intention being to subject the guilty person to death purely and simply. The executioner, through lack of experience, could make decapitation into a frightful torture, and this is what we in fact apprehend.

"We accordingly submit to the National Assembly those circumstances which seem to us to make necessary a decree relative to the method of applying Article 3 of the *Code Pénal*." [1]

The death sentence referred to had been passed on Nicolas-Jacques Pelletier the previous December for a little matter of robbery with violence, and the Tribunal's and the *Directoire's* impatience on his behalf helped provide him in due course with the distinction of being the guillotine's first official victim. He was further assisted towards this sinister immortality by the Minister of Justice, who, nagged at by his colleagues, also took it out on the President of the Assembly:

"I am obliged to submit", he wrote on March 3rd, "to the urgent attention of the National Assembly a point requiring an immediate decision and concerning which I would nonetheless be reluctant to speak, were it not that the need to carry out the judgements of the courts, were it not that humanity and the importance of not arousing the ferocity of public opinion obliged me to allude to it once and for all: I refer to the method of execution.

"Our new laws require that the death sentence should involve nothing but the deprivation of life. They provide for

[1] See Pichon, op. cit.

decapitation as the penalty most in conformity with this principle. In this they are mistaken—or, at any rate, if such an end is to be reached, a form must be sought and made uniform which will meet that requirement, and enlightened humanity must perfect the art of giving death in such a way. . . ." [1]

Bedevilled, the Assembly was at last moved to concern itself with the problem, and Dr Antoine Louis, the secretary of the *Académie Chirurgical*, was requested to report on the possibility of manufacturing a machine which could be relied on to relieve enlightened humanity of its enemies without wounding its sensibilities.

"A noble old man of sixty-nine full of enthusiasm for his art", [2] "the glory of the *Académie Chirurgical*", [3] renowned—in a rather limited *milieu*—for having perfected innumerable surgical implements (although never so radical a one as that on which he was now called to pronounce), Dr Louis was a humanitarian like everyone else. Not, however, quite so old-maidishly as Dr Guillotin; he was, in fact, possessed of a bleak humour and a dissecting-room cynicism which made him—even apart from his professional qualifications—an ideal choice for the job.

There is an anecdote [4] to the effect that his consulting-room door carried a placard informing callers that "those who visit me, honour me; those who do not, please me", but this suggestion of troglodytic seclusion was only a little affectation of the great man's. He was, as a matter of fact, rather a gregarious old gentleman and his Sunday evening parties grouped together a horde of celebrated individuals. [5] Among the eminent

[1] Ibid.

[2] See Chéreau, op. cit.

[3] See Lacassagne, op. cit.

[4] See *Biographie moderne ou galérie historique, civile, militaire, politique, littéraire et judiciaire* (Chez Alexis Eymery, Paris, 1816).

[5] An account of these soirées was written by Dr Louis' grand-nephew, Emile Begin, under the title *Trilogie révolutionnaire*. It has never been published and the manuscript was made available to me by its owner, M. Pierre D'Espezel.

medical men usually to be found at these "*Dominicales*" were Cabanis, Percy and Lacretelle; literature was represented by Crébillon *fils*, Goldoni and Diderot, politics by Robespierre and, significantly, Roederer; and the gatherings were habitually presided over by the sprightly Sophie Arnoult. It is appropriate to the epoch that the guillotine should have known this connection with a veritable *salon*.

On March 17th, 1792,[1] Dr Louis submitted his *Avis motivé sur le mode de la Décolation* (*sic*). The document not only represents the first practical steps towards creation of the guillotine but demonstrates that in Louis had been found a figure worthy of the grandguignolesque possibilities:

"The Legislation Committee has done me the honour of consulting me about two letters written to the National Assembly concerning the implementation of Article 3 under Heading 1 of the *Code Pénal*, which stipulates that: Every person condemned to the death penalty shall have his head severed. In these letters, the Minister of Justice and the *Directoire* of the Department of Paris, in view of the representations made to them, consider it urgently necessary to determine precisely the means of carrying out the law, fearing that if a faulty method or lack of experience or maladdress rendered the punishment horrible for the victim and the spectators, the people might, out of humanity, behave unjustly and cruelly towards the executioner, a contingency which it is important to avoid.[2]

"I consider that the representations are fair and the fears well-founded. Both experience and reason demonstrate that the method hitherto used to sever the head of a criminal exposes him to a punishment more hideous than the mere

---

[1] Begin gives the date of this document as March 7th, but for various reasons this seems unlikely.

[2] Dr Louis may have had in mind the unhappy end of the swordsman, Fluraut, in 1517. Having badly bungled an execution, he was chased by the shocked aficionados and took refuge in a house which the mob burnt over him. Poor Fluraut was not the only executioner whose lack of skill led to this sort of horseplay.

deprivation of life, which is the explicit intention of the law: to meet this wish, it is necessary that the execution be carried out instantaneously and at one stroke: all too many examples prove how difficult this is to achieve.

"One may well recall at this point what was observed at the decapitation of M. de Lally; he was on his knees, his eyes bandaged; the executioner struck on the nape of the neck; the stroke did not succeed in removing the head, nor could it have done so.[1] The body, with nothing to prevent its falling, was thrown forward, and three or four slashes of the sword were required before the head was finally separated from the body: this *hacherie*, if one may coin the term, could only be contemplated with horror.

"In Germany, the executioners are more experienced owing to the frequency of this type of despatching, mainly due to the fact that persons of the female sex, no matter what their social level, are subjected to no other form of capital punishment: nonetheless, the perfect execution is not often achieved, despite the precaution taken in certain places of maintaining the victim seated in a chair.

"In Denmark, there are two positions and two instruments for decapitation. The execution which one might term *honorific* is carried out with a sabre; the criminal kneels, his eyes are bandaged, his hands free. If the punishment is to be ignominious, the victim, bound, is laid face downwards and his head is cut off with an axe.

"Everyone knows that cutting instruments have little or no effect when they strike perpendicularly; when one studies them under the microscope one sees that they are only more or less fine saws, that one must saw the object to be cut. One could not decapitate at a single stroke with an axe or blade of which the cutting edge was straight; but with a convex

---

[1] This assertion seems too *ex cathedra* by half; there exists a series of photographs showing a Chinese swordsman—with his victim in just the position described by Louis—achieving a decapitation at one stroke without the least difficulty in the world.

cutting edge, as in the old battle-axes, the blow dealt is not per-pendicular except in the middle of the segment; the instrument, as the blade penetrates further into the parts divided, has an oblique sawing action at the sides and must therefore fulfil its function.

"When we consider the structure of the neck, of which the spinal column is the centre, being composed of a number of bones so connected that no joint can be located, it is not pos-sible to be sure of a prompt and perfect separation if the task is entrusted to an agent likely to vary in skill for moral or physical reasons; it is absolutely necessary, if the process is to be sure, that it should depend on unvarying mechanical means of which the force and effect can also be determined. This is the view which has been adopted in England; [1] the criminal's body is placed face-downwards between two posts with a cross-piece at the top from which a convex axe is allowed to fall by means of a trigger onto the man's neck. The top of the instrument should be sufficiently strong and heavy to act effectively like the ram used for pile-driving: it is well known that its force increases according to the height from which it falls.

"It is easy to have such a machine built, the effect of which will be unfailing; decapitation will be carried out in an instant, in conformity with the spirit and the intention of the new law; it will be easy to try it out on corpses or even on a living sheep. It will then be seen whether the victim's head should be held in place by a crescent-shaped cross-piece which will encircle the neck at the base of the skull, the tips or projections of this crescent being fastened by king-pins under the scaffold: this apparatus, should it be deemed necessary, would induce no sensation and would scarcely be noticed at all." [2]

Ingenious Dr Louis! The machine thus (one feels) almost

[1] An oddly misleading statement: decapitation by mechanical means was never general in England, and at the time of Dr Louis' report had long ceased to be used in Halifax.

[2] See Pichon, op. cit.

"The Maiden"

PLATE III

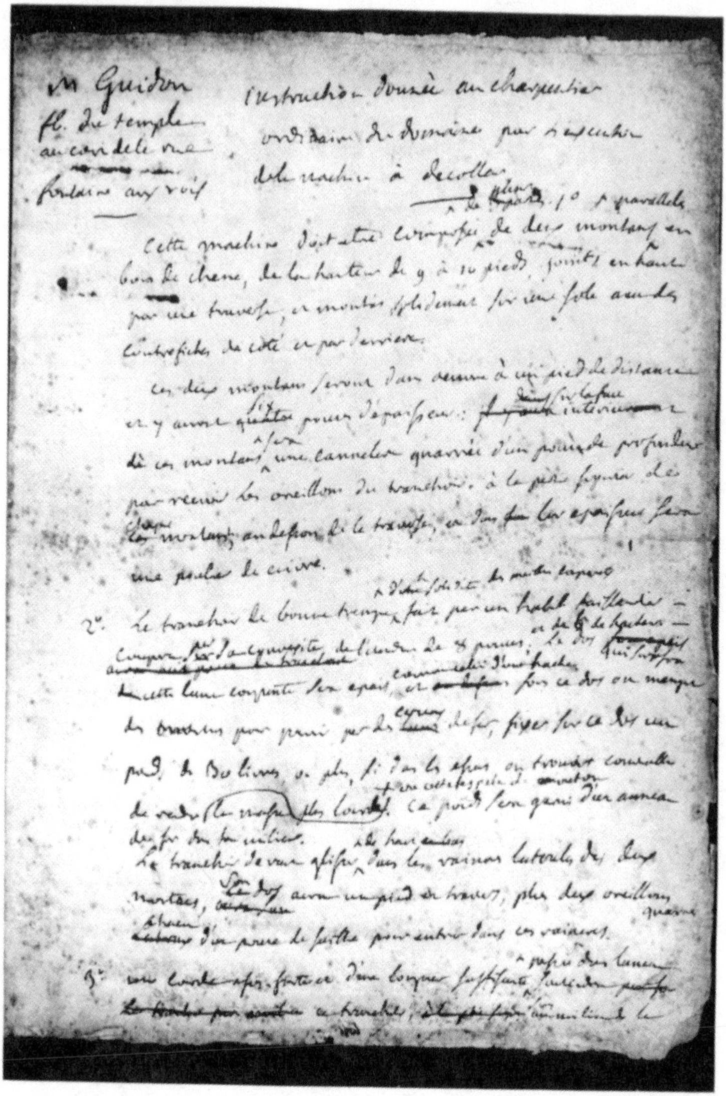

Pierre D'Espezel

Dr Antoine Louis' instructions to the carpenter for the construction of the first guillotine

PLATE IV

casually proposed differs not at all in essentials from that which today hides in the Santé prison. And yet, with strange modesty, with an indignation quite incomprehensible in such a merry old cynic, the Doctor declined the compliment implicit in one of the popular names originally bestowed on the implement:

"My part in the matter," he assured a friend, "and I consider it an act of humanity, was limited to correcting the shape of the blade and making it oblique so that it would cut cleanly and achieve its object. My enemies then tried . . . to give the fatal machine the name of 'Little Louison' or 'Louisette' which, however, they were unable to substitute for that of 'guillotine'."[1]

The austere historical facts do nothing to sustain the disclaimer: the Legislation Committee was ravished by the results of the surgeon's meditations, observing in a letter reproduced by M. Begin that "the reflexions born of your humanity and your profound anatomical knowledge have been adopted by the Committee . . . (and) you thus have the merit of having benefited humanity even when the law's blade strikes the head of the guilty." Could any affirmation of Dr Louis' intimate involvement be more explicit?

Whether encouraged by this tribute, or whether—like Dr Guillotin—acting out of sheer spontaneous enthusiasm for good works, Dr Louis henceforward would seem to have subordinated all his interests to the captivating problem in hand. For the next month, the spry old gentleman was busy with his hobby-horse, discussing it with the guests at those urbane Sunday evening symposia of his, corresponding with different administrative officials, firing off grim little witticisms in sign of his enjoyment, and, finally, handing a really detailed description which he had drawn up to M. Guidon, the carpenter accustomed to provide the State with its scaffolds:

"This machine should be composed of several parts.

[1] See René Desgenettes: *Souvenirs de la fin du XVIII siècle* (Firmin Did o Frères, Paris, 1835).

"1. Two parallel uprights in oak ten feet high, joined at the top by a cross-piece and solidly mounted on a base with supporting braces at the sides and back.

"These two uprights will be a foot apart on the inside and will be six inches thick; on the inner sides of these uprights will be longitudinal square grooves, one inch in depth, to take the side-pieces of a blade. At the top of each of these uprights, beneath the cross-bar, a brass pulley will be countersunk.

"2. The blade, well tempered, with the solidity of the best cleavers and made by a competent cutler, will cut on account of its convexity. This cutting edge will measure eight inches across and six in height. The top of this blade will be as thick as an axe; beneath this top edge, the metal-worker will make openings so that a thirty-pound weight or larger can be attached to it by means of iron bands; should it prove desirable during the trials to increase the heaviness of this 'ram', the latter will be furnished with an iron ring in the middle.

"The blade-holder must slide down in the grooves of the two uprights; its top will measure a foot across, plus two square tenons projecting one inch to fit in these grooves.

"3. A sufficiently strong and long rope will be threaded through the ring and will maintain the knife-holder under the upper cross-bar: each end of this rope will be threaded from the inside over the corresponding pulley and will be fastened on the outside at the foot of each upright.

"4. The wooden block on which the victim's neck is to be placed will be eight inches high and four inches thick. Its base will be a foot wide, that is to say the distance between the two uprights; a detachable bolt will pierce each upright in order to hold the said block at each side of the base. The upper part of this block will be only eight inches wide. It will have a slit across its upper surface to take the cutting edge of the convex blade. Accordingly, the lateral inside grooves of the two uprights should not extend lower than this slit in order that the block shall not be cut by the blade. The top of the block will be slightly scooped out so that the victim's neck can be comfortably lodged.

"5. But to hold the head down and ensure that it is not lifted at the moment of execution, an iron crescent, in the shape of a horse-shoe with thoroughly rounded edges, should encircle the victim's neck above the nape at the foot of the skull where the scalp ends. The extremities of this crescent, reasonably extended, should be pierced so as to be held in place by a bolt passing through the beginning of the upper part of the block which is four inches thick.

"The victim, laid face-downwards, will have his chest supported by his elbows, and his neck will be placed without difficulty in the scooped-out part of the block. If everything has been properly arranged, the executioner standing by the machine will be able to hold the two ends of the rope supporting the blade-holder and, on his releasing them simultaneously, this instrument falling down from a height will, by its weight and acceleration of speed, separate the head from the body in the twinkling of an eye.

"Should there be a few errors of detail herein", the Doctor ended, "they could easily be rectified by even the stupidest builder." [1]

Was M. Guidon, that important functionary, offended by these concluding words? At all events, just when things seemed to be really under way and all the humanitarians at last able to relax momentarily before tackling mankind's next problem, Guidon introduced a maddening hitch. Late in March he submitted his estimate [2] for the construction of the implement—5,660 *livres*.[3] Even the stupidest builder . . .

It was intolerable, impossible, and Guidon's justification of

[1] See Fleischmann, op cit.
[2] See Pichon, op. cit.
[3] Approximately £226 at the then rate of exchange.

the figure insultingly unconvincing. He would need to pay his workmen at a special rate, he explained, because of their prejudice (which Dr Louis qualified as "absurd but difficult to destroy"[1]) against such disagreeable work. That such a prejudice existed in that epoch of universal sensibility could not be denied, but it would be a poor sort of philosopher who could not resolve a conflict between the god of reason and Mammon; and why this sudden hostility towards the positively enjoyable guillotine among artisans who had never balked at throwing together the grisly gibbets of the bad old days?

Yet there it was; Dr Louis passed the news on to M. Roederer, feeling it necessary to observe that "you will be appalled, perhaps, by the price which he (Guidon) asks for building the machine".[2] M. Roederer, with all the bureaucrat's unconcern for the spending of public monies, was not, as it happened, in the least appalled at that stage; indeed, he replied that he was happy to "authorise the Sieur Guidon to build the machine on the terms and at the price he has mentioned".[3] At the same time, he hinted that he and the Doctor needed a little chat and announced his intention of dropping by at Louis' residence a few days later. Perhaps Dr Louis would be good enough to arrange for his professional colleagues, Drs Lacuée, Broussonnet and Guillotin, to be present at 9 a.m. on the due day; while if M. Guidon and M. Sanson could join them an hour later, so much the better.[4]

Was it at this meeting that M. Roederer, piqued somehow by Guidon, decided that the latter's terms were exorbitant? We have no way of knowing; but certainly it was not long after that M. Roederer was writing to the Finance Minister, M. Clavière, to express his stupefaction at Guidon's avarice, adding that a number of craftsmen had "offered to build the machine at a considerably lower price . . . only asking that

¹ See Fleischmann, op. cit.   ² Ibid.
³ Begin MS.   ⁴ Ibid.

they should not be required to sign an estimate because of their wish to remain unknown to the public".[1]

The delay which Guidon's intransigence would necessarily cause was an exasperating circumstance; busybodies of all sorts were pestering the exhausted Roederer without respite, Judge Moreau of the Second Criminal Tribunal, for instance, apostrophising him almost at that moment "in the name of humanity and the public good" to get a machine under way.[2] But 5,660 *livres*! With the bewildering inconsistency of the *rond-de-cuir*, Roederer had abruptly chosen to regard the sum as no longer merely another exaction for the public purse to endure but as a fortune which personal enemies were trying to extract from his private purse. Pelletier, in the condemned cell, had managed to wait three months so far; in the circumstances, if he were any kind of patriot at all, he could not object to the postponement of his execution a little longer. The whole thing, in a manner of speaking, was being done in his interests anyway.

Some time before, indefatigably interested in perfecting this latest surgical instrument, Dr Louis had addressed a characteristic letter to the *Procureur général syndic*,[3] informing him that "a German harpsichord-maker has felt he could employ his genius in regard to the beheading machine. I do not know him, but I applaud his industry. The victim would be neither bound nor laid down. His head, in a pillory, would be infallibly severed by an oblique cut. I esteem it a duty to send you this mechanic and a pleasure to assure you, Monsieur, of my respectful feelings towards you."[4]

---

[1] See Taschereau, op. cit.
[2] Ibid.
[3] See Fleischmann, op. cit.
[4] M. Begin affirms that Schmidt first entered the history as piano-teacher to Roederer's daughters. When the *Procureur général syndic* was seeking a substitute for Guidon, he at once thought of Schmidt—whose gifts as piano-maker he rather mysteriously equated with a capacity to construct beheading machines. Indignantly Schmidt pointed out that he was an executant, not an executioner, and only by threatening him with deportation unless he complied was Roederer able to obtain his services. It is a pity that all the evidence contradicts this delicious fantasy.

The German harpsichord-maker was Tobias Schmidt, "who sometimes abandons this art to devote himself to discoveries of benefit to humanity" [1] (how insufferably disinterested *everyone* tried to be in that age!). He was, it is clear, an engaging fantast who provided an admirable foil for Louis and who must have endlessly delighted that saturnine creature. At a later stage in what was evidently a singularly grotesque career, he invented "a hydraulic machine with which one can descend in water to any depth whatever"; a patent chimney; a ghastly sort of primitive pianola which produced the effects of viola, violin and 'cello, and a whole madhouse of similar contrivances.[2] In view of the shabby treatment which he was later to receive in connection with his activities as manufacturer of a head-chopping machine, it is pleasant to be able to record that his other activities provided him with a considerable income, so that towards 1800, having fallen in love with a glamorous dancer, "*le grossier soupirant*" (as one writer unkindly terms him) was able to steal her from a fascinating but impecunious army officer.[3]

Confronted with Guidon's impudent cupidity, Roederer called Schmidt to mind. Negotiations were rapid, friendly and commonsensible. On April 10th, 1792, Roederer and Schmidt reached a happy accord: 960 francs was to cover the cost of manufacturing the machine, the sum moreover providing for a leather bag in which to dispose of the severed head—a practical consideration. In his official capacity as furnisher of scaffolds, M. Guidon, despite the ferocious extortions he had attempted, was retained to supply the high platform on which Schmidt's creation was to be erected.

As Dr Louis had already indicated, Schmidt possessed a heart-warming enthusiasm for this mechanical novelty, so much so that he had actually roughed out a design of his own (see

[1] See *Le Moniteur*, 8 vend., An III.
[2] See Chéreau, op. cit.
[3] See Dr Cabanès: *Le Cabinet secret de l'histoire*; 4th series (Albin Michel, Paris, 1905).

Plate V); and even though it was not his [1] but Dr Louis' plan which he was charged to construct, he applied himself with such pretty devotion that less than a week later, Louis was able to inform M. Roederer [2] that "the Sieur Schmidt, maker of musical instruments, is busy by your orders with an instrument having quite another purpose".

[1] Louis du Bois in his *Recherches historiques et physiologiques sur la guillotine* (Chez France, Paris, 1834) contends that this design was actually the work of Laquiante, *Commissaire du roi* in the department of the Bas-Rhin, and merely built for him in model form by Schmidt, but there seems to be no evidence in support of the claim. On the other hand, M. Quentin-Bauchart (op. cit.) asserts that the design was indeed by Schmidt but submitted by him to Laquiante for forwarding to the appropriate authorities, which appears altogether more likely.

[2] See Fleischmann, op. cit.

CHAPTER FIVE

WHILE corresponding with Roederer, Dr Louis was simultaneously in brisk communication with the chief surgeon of Bicêtre, Dr Cullerier, regarding arrangements for trials to be held within the next few days. On Saturday, April 12th, 1792, he wrote to this distinguished associate that "the mechanic charged with the construction of the beheading machine will not be ready to try it out until Tuesday. I have just written to the *Procureur général syndic* so that he may instruct the person who must operate it in public and in real earnest to present himself on Tuesday at ten o'clock at the place decided on for the trials. I have informed the *Directoire* of the department with what zeal you have taken up the general wish in regard to this distressing matter. . . ." [1]

The establishment of Bicêtre, just outside Paris, was a sort of combined prison, public hospital and old peoples' home, and had been chosen by Louis as the site for his tests presumably, if one may judge from the correspondence which passed between him and the chief surgeon of the place, because of the certainty of a supply of cadavers. Or again, it is possible that he was attracted by the fact that Dr Cullerier had glimmerings of a charnel humour not unlike his own:

"Monsieur," wrote Dr Cullerier as soon as he had received his colleague's discreetly flattering note, "you will find at Bicêtre all the facilities you may wish in order to carry out the trial of a machine which humanity cannot contemplate without a shudder but which justice and the welfare of society

[1] See Chéreau, op. cit.

make necessary. I will keep the corpses of such unfortunates as may die between today and Monday. I will arrange the theatre in a suitable fashion. If, as I imagine, the level of the ceiling is inadequate for the height of the machine, I can make use of a small isolated courtyard beside the theatre. Your choice of the Hospital of Bicêtre, Monsieur, I consider a most pleasant attention; but it would be even more so if you would consent to accept the sort of simple and frugal meal which a bachelor can offer. . . ." [1]

What an enchanting meal it must have been, with Louis and Cullerier swapping slaughter-house jests for the benefit of the headsman and the other convivial ghouls! But who were they? According to Fleischmann,[2] Sanson was accompanied by his two brothers and his son, functioning in the capacity of assistant-executioners, while the medical profession was represented by Louis, Cullerier, Cabanis, Philippe Pinel and Guillotin. M. Quentin-Bauchart, however, remarks [3] that there is no reason to believe that Guillotin was present—and indeed one would have expected him to have held fastidiously aloof from the coarse practical application of his principles. M. Begin [4] says nothing of Cabanis and Pinel nor of Sanson's relatives; he agrees as to the presence of his great-uncle, Cullerier and Guillotin, and adds three other sawbones for good measure—Lacretelle, Nysten and Maret. Moreover, he insists, a number of journalists and Hospital personnel turned up uninvited for the trials until the total number of spectators was around about forty. Dr Cabanis,[5] who really was in a position to know, maddeningly contents himself with alluding to "a certain number", and M. Lenotre [6] chooses to avoid the whole issue.

[1] An unpublished letter from the collection of M. Pierre D'Espezel.
[2] See Fleischmann, op. cit.
[3] See Quentin-Bauchart, op. cit.
[4] See Begin MS.
[5] See P. J. G. Cabanis: *Oeuvres complètes* (Bossanges frères & Firmin Didot, Paris, 1823–5).
[6] See Lenotre, op. cit.

The same confusion exists in regard to the involuntary guests of honour—the corpses so civilly made available by Dr Cullerier to try out the new gadget. In reporting to Roederer,[1] Louis speaks of three cadavers having been used; in subsequently reporting to the *Procureur général syndic* of the Department of the Seine-et-Oise,[2] Roederer alludes to five; M. Begin—always large-minded—over-bids with eleven.

Finally, one cannot even be definite as to the date of the entertainment. On Saturday, April 12th, 1792, as already mentioned, Dr Louis named "next Tuesday" as the day—i.e. the 15th; but on April 18th, Roederer addressed a note to Louis [3] requesting information on "the experiment . . . which took place yesterday"—i.e. the 17th. M. Begin's manuscript, which can always be relied on to complicate still further the already complicated, gives the date as the 14th and sends the conscientious researcher tottering towards despair by insisting that there were two distinct tests on two different days, not including a preliminary try-out in Guidon's backyard.

Setting aside M. Begin for the moment and ignoring the purely social problem of who was present, it seems reasonable to go by Dr Louis' own letters since he, at any rate, was unquestionably present. On this basis, it would seem that on Tuesday, April 15th, 1792, three carcasses were placed on the *bascule* and expeditiously decapitated—so expeditiously that Sanson is said to have remarked in dolorous commendation that it was "a fine machine—so long as its facility is not abused".[4] On April 19th, Dr Louis, with restrained rapture, informed M. Roederer that "the trials of the Sieur Schmidt's machine were carried out on Tuesday at Bicêtre on three corpses. It decapitated these so cleanly that one was astonished by the force and the celerity of its action. . . ." [5]

[1] See Fleischmann, op. cit.   [2] See Taschereau, op. cit.
[3] Ibid.   [4] See Cabanès, op. cit.
[5] See Fleischmann, op. cit.

The Doctor's laconic treatment of so historic an event is a sad disappointment, and there is no doubt that M. Begin's version—however suspicious one may be as to its accuracy—is vastly more worthy of the occasion. It was on the afternoon of the 11th, he tells us, that Guidon set up the new machine in the courtyard of his workshops.[1] Dr Louis was not himself present but was represented by that up-and-coming young medical man, Dr Nysten; and, instead of human corpses, two or three living sheep and calves had been sent along from the abattoirs: "their necks", M. Begin observes, "presented more or less the same degree of resistance as would a human neck", and, assuming that M. Begin is correct, the tests indicated that the betterment of condemned men's lot was appreciably nearer, for the creatures' heads were sliced off with remarkable ease.

But whatever resemblance there might be between a sheep's neck and a man's, Dr Louis could only be satisfied after observing the effect of his machine on authentically human flesh, and (always according to M. Begin) on April 14th, this perfectionism was duly gratified at Bicêtre, the trials being conducted "with decency and piety". With a pretty sense of precedence, the headsman began with the women and children among his corpses, and their delicate necks were severed as easily as if they had been sheep or calves; two male bodies were decapitated with equal ease; the observers, inspecting the neat severances as the executioner passed the heads one by one across to them, discreetly rejoiced. But suddenly, dramatically—a hitch! A brace of male necks resisted the blade; its force was used up in slicing through the vertebrae and—"a horrible sight"—the heads remained attached to the bodies by a few shreds of cartilage. "Nonetheless," remarks M. Begin reassuringly, "it was certain that each of these individuals, had they been living, would have at once ceased to exist. There

---

[1] Lenotre (op. cit.) fixes the location of this site as the Cour du Commerce, rue Saint-André-des-Arts.

was no question of uncertainty as to life or death . . . but a concern with, to use an old surgical term, the *jucundum*, the satisfactory *appearance* of the operation." When a third male corpse's "Herculean muscular structure" was unaffected by the fall of the blade three times repeated, the judges' Hippocratic integrity obliged them to admit that the *jucundum* simply would not do.

Louis meditated briefly and recommended that the uprights be increased in height so that the blade would descend with greater force and that the shape of the blade [1] be altered; Cullerier, Nysten and Guillotin were in accord and the last of these there and then sketched out a revised version.

"After so melancholy a scene," says M. Begin, "no one was inclined for lunch." The loss of appetite is creditable to all concerned, but Dr Cullerier was naturally anxious that his "simple and frugal" meal should not be wasted. With ready tact, he "proposed that his guests should visit the gardens and park of the Château . . . which had lost nothing of their aristocratic charm. The April foliage, of so tenderly verdant a hue, enhanced by the sunshine and already flecked with buds and sweet-smelling flowers, delighted the eye and re-placed with happier reflections the gloomy thoughts which filled all present. After an hour's stroll, during which the chap-lain carried out the burial of the corpses, the company returned to Cullerier's residence where a meal was served which had no relationship to the food shortage or to the tragic picture which had earlier been before all eyes. . . . Full justice was done to the capon and to the wines of an excellent cellar. . . .''

Promptly on his return to Paris, Guillotin, and Schmidt, paid a visit to a tool-maker who promised that the newly-conceived blade would be ready within three days, and on April 19th Guidon went out to Bicêtre to fix it in position. On April 21st the machine was again tried out, and this time

---

[1] M. Begin gives no indication as to the shape of the original blade, and of Guillotin's amended version says only that it was "bevelled".

it functioned *à merveille*. Three corpses had been carefully
selected from the military hospitals "in order to obtain, if possible, really well-built men who had died in an accident or of
some short illness which had not caused them to grow thin".
A suicide, a duel between two Alsatian gunners (the loser only
was of interest to the researchers) and an apparently epic drinking bout had providentially occurred in the preceding days
and provided "three corpses of Herculean dimensions whose
vertebrae and skin were forced to yield, humiliated, to Dr
Guillotin's all-powerful blade".

Dr Louis was not present at this second test, and M. Begin
shrewdly asks whether his absence was not perhaps deliberate.
Moreover, "in choosing Guillotin to rectify the apparatus and
make the final preparatory tests, did he (Louis) wish to get the
business off his hands and withdraw from the whole matter ?"

Begin's saga of these ghastly drolls is supported by no
evidence whatever and, in a number of particulars, is demon-
strably inaccurate; but in suggesting that his great-uncle was
eager to sidle out of the history he is certainly correct. A more
than Oriental self-effacement seems to have developed in all
those connected with the guillotine, and Guillotin and Louis
vie with each other in seeking to disqualify themselves from
receiving the thanks of grateful humanity.

From very early in the story, according to M. Begin,
humorous guests at the "*Dominicales*" had begun to tease Dr
Louis about his macabre activities, and one of them, the poet
Laujon, had wittily addressed some versicles to him in celebra-
tion thereof:

> *Loin des caresses,*
> *Des gentillesses,*
> *De mes drôlesses,*
> *Cora, Marthe et Suzon;*
> *Dans cette ivresse*
> *Glisse sans cesse*
> *Un noir poison*

J'aime bien mieux Louison,
  Landerinette
  Quoique coquette
  Elle est honnête
  Constante et coetera
  Landerinette,
  Landerina.

  Sa gorge est nue,
  Son baiser tue,
  Le sang afflue
Et l'on se voit mourir.
  Charmante étreinte
  Sans huile sainte,
  Sans larme feinte
Il est doux de franchir
  Landerinette
  Cette vedette
  Bouche muette
Sans entendre un hola,
  Landerinette,
  Landerina.

  Vive Louisette
  Digne fillette
  Tendre et folette
Du docte Antoine Louis;
  Elle m'enchante
  Chacun la vante
  Sans bien ni rente
Personne n'a son prix
  Landerinette
  Quelle toilette!
  Ah! c'est sa fête

Courons ce festin-là,
Landerinette,
Landerina.

Mlle Arnoult was reputedly enchanted by this jest at the expense of her old friend, and doubtless the other members of the *cénacle* shared her enjoyment. Dr Louis himself was able to control whatever guffaws may have risen in him: he missed no opportunity of insisting on his remoteness from the whole sordid affair. To M. Desgenettes, as we have seen, he gave an assurance that he had done no more than provide a helping hand to those really responsible; the allusion, in his report to Roederer, to "the Sieur Schmidt's machine" was followed, in the same letter, by an unequivocal reference to Schmidt as the implement's "ingenious inventor", and a note sent to Sophie Arnoult [1] speaks, with magisterial good-humour, of "this misnamed young lady (the Louisette) whose father I am not".

But one cannot turn out that sort of toy and forever escape from the responsibility. Even though wretched little Dr Guillotin was resolutely fathered with the credit in the minds of the general public, the documents are there to prove that it was indeed Dr Louis' grisly aptitude which gave birth to the device, and nothing could be more unambiguous than Roederer's allusion (at a later stage of the history) to Schmidt's effrontery in seeking a patent "for a machine of which he is not in reality the inventor, and to which he only made a few alterations on Dr Louis' description". [2]

Among all those who have studied the facts, Dr Louis' authorship of the guillotine is disputed by no one but himself.

[1] Quoted by Begin.   [2] See Taschereau, op. cit.

CHAPTER SIX

IT is very sad, but contemporary observers were blind to the high historical importance of that first experimental machine tried out at Bicêtre and none of them bothered to note the precise details of its appearance. One might have expected better things of the droll Dr Louis, but, no, not even he thought to leave its portrait or to arrange for its eventual lodgement in a technological museum. There is a similar lack of information concerning the improved and corrected model which was used to remove Pelletier's head at the first actual execution by a guillotine; while even such rumoured oddities as the lightweight machine especially built in 1794 for convenient installation in sick-rooms where the guilty lay helpless [1] were not thought important enough to merit conservation. Most tragically of all, that formidable mechanism with which the King himself was executed has likewise disappeared, its picture undrawn—or, at all events, those artists who portrayed the scene felt free to indulge all sorts of whimsy when sketching the structure. In any case, what picture could compensate for the loss of the machine itself?

There is an improbable anecdote [2] in which the comte O'Mahony shelters from a storm in a deserted building near Auch; he seats himself on a heap of planks; arriving at his destination he learns that he had sheltered in the home of the executioner, that he had perched on the remnants of the very

---

[1] Communication from the Feldhaus-Archiv. Wilhelmshaven.
[2] Quoted by Fleischmann, op. cit., and others.

Projet
de Machine à décapiter
proposé d'abord par Schmidt.

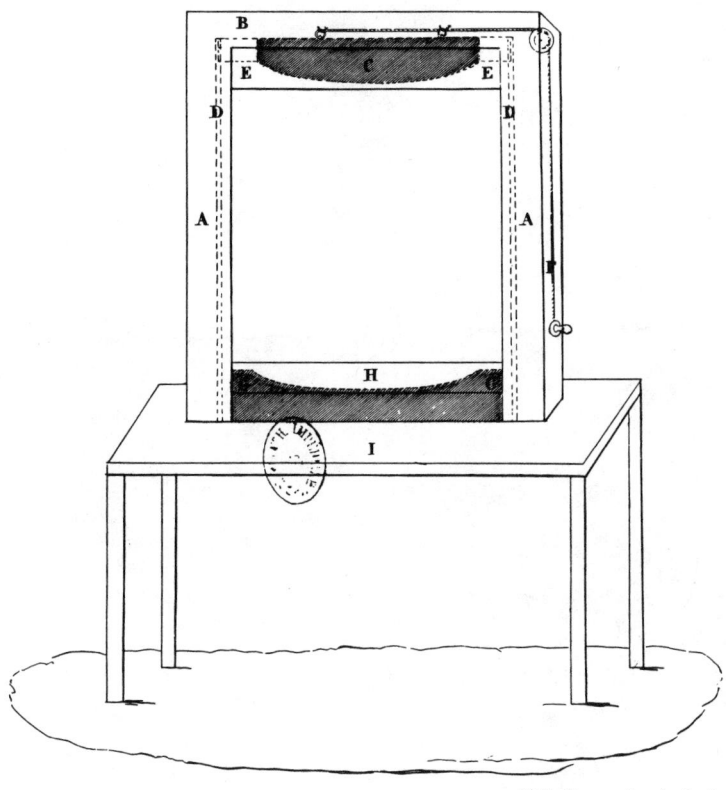

A decapitating machine devised by Tobias Schmidt

PLATE V

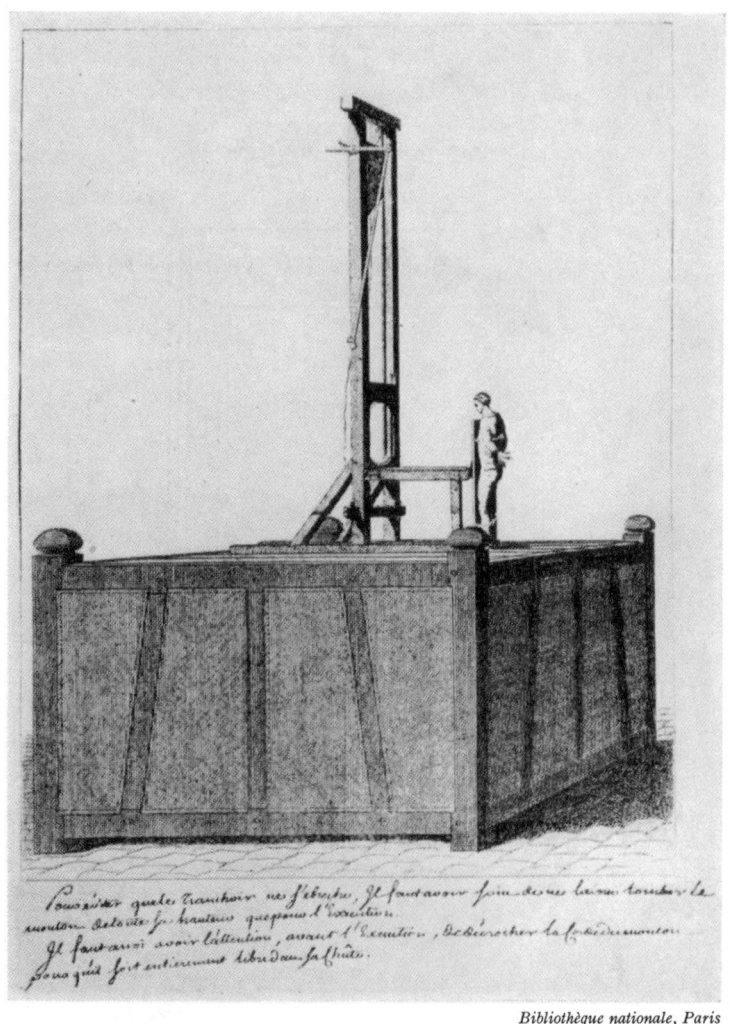

The earliest authentic portrayal of a guillotine. Sketch accompanying each of the machines supplied to the provinces in 1792

PLATE VI

guillotine which decapitated Louis XVI. And the journalist, Hugues le Roux, submits a yet more picturesque tale: [1] the King's guillotine was exiled to the penal settlement in Guiana; diminished, demeaned, having only plebeian necks to deal with, it was still functioning there, says M. le Roux, in 1891.

Mme Roch, widow of that distinguished headsman, Nicolas Roch, claimed to know the whereabouts of the blade, if not the entire implement, which had destroyed the King.[2] On March 17th, 1893, she wrote to a rather specialised collector in Brussels, M. Dubois, who some twenty years before had purchased a guillotine from her husband. Now Mme Roch offered a stack of positive treasures for his consideration, including a number of blades, among them that which had severed the necks of the King and of Marie-Antoinette. Cautious M. Dubois asked for details, and on April 4th Mme Roch explained that her husband had acquired what she neatly termed the "*fonds de magasin*" from his predecessor, Heindreicht; this forlorn detritus included the great blade, piously preserved by Roch throughout his life. When he died, the widow mentioned in passing, his replacement, Deibler, had claimed these keepsakes as perquisites of the office, but he "did not want to pay me . . . I therefore removed everything which belonged to me, including the blades. . . . He complained to the Ministry and I was summoned and asked to deliver the blades to the Archives. But the State didn't want to pay me either. So I said that I hadn't got them and that I didn't know what my husband had done with them. . . ."

The story furnishes a quaint glimpse into the lives of the executioners but seems inconclusive as a means of identifying the regicidal blade, although M. Dubois was satisfied and the purchase completed.

But did he get what he hoped? Or did it go—had it already

[1] See *Le Figaro*, July 20th, 1891.
[2] See *l'Illustration*, December 18th, 1909.

gone—to Madame Tussaud's in London? Certainly *a* guillotine
was acquired by her establishment in 1854 when Clément
Sanson, grandson of the King's executioner, came to terms
with M. Joseph Tussaud. Clément himself had ceased to occupy
the post of executioner (the unpleasant details of his fall from
grace are given elsewhere in the present work) but had
managed to retain one of the guillotines in his keeping. Or
more or less in his keeping, for it was currently in pawn and
he without funds to redeem it. On March 27th, 1854, M.
Tussaud entered in his note-book, "Paid to Sampson [*sic*] for
Guillotine—£110-0-0", and on April 4th paid over another
£110 to the pawnbroker and returned to London with his
fearful acquisition.[1]

To the student of decapitation, however, it is the loss of the
prototype, the infant guillotine of Bicêtre, which is ultimately
heart-breaking. Clearly it cannot have differed very much
from the first guillotine of which a reliable portrait exists (see
Plate VI), but a number of fanciers have helped raise a suspicion
that there were some important variations. The blade, for
example: when was the familiar slanting form first introduced?
Dr Louis' original plan called for a convex model; the shape
employed today (and which is shown in the above-mentioned
sketch) may have replaced this before the Bicêtre tests, between
the time of the tests and the execution of Pelletier (unlikely,
however, despite M. Begin, in view of the short time available)
or at some point after that execution.[2] A teasing problem.

As to the machine used on Pelletier, it was certainly taller
than the modern guillotine, was painted a becoming red, and
was mounted on a high scaffold. Once drawn to the top of the
frame, the blade was held in place by a primitive attachment
consisting of a pivoted lever on one of the uprights supporting

[1] Communication from Madame Tussaud's, London. The machine in
question was destroyed by fire—along with the documents of authentication
—in 1925, the blade and part of the *mouton* alone being saved.

[2] This is the opinion of R. P. Réveille-Parise: *Étude biographique: Guillotin,
Joseph-Ignace* (Imprimerie de Panckoucke, Paris, 1851).

an arm which projected from the blade's accompanying weight.

But it is impossible to give an accurate description of the early guillotines, even apart from the Bicêtre and Pelletier models, for the simple reason that for a long time there was no settled design in use throughout France. As a minor indication, when the guillotine of the abominable Javogues came up for public auction in 1909, it was noted that the two uprights were surmounted by carved Phrygian bonnets,[1] but whether such emblematic touches were common cannot be established.

Again, as late as 1811, Henry Sanson, from his ripe knowledge sending some friendly counsel to his opposite number at Liège, remarked that "elsewhere (than in Paris), the body is allowed to fall through a hole in the scaffold and into a sort of little tomb. Each Department does as it thinks best in this regard. . . ."[2]

Finally, there was a complex lack of uniformity about the blades, even after the design for the Paris implement had been ostensibly settled. One commentator[3] assures us that it was initially built in convex form, as recommended by Dr Louis; then made concave (presumably in conformity with Schmidt's —or Laquiante's—design); next shaped like a wide sword point (on the direct advice of the King himself); then given its habitual oblique edge; and that all of these quaint cleavers might be seen functioning in the provinces as late as 1850.

The contention has been vigorously denied,[4] but in that

[1] See l'Illustration, December 11th, 1909.

[2] The letter, dated October 27th, 1811, is quoted by Georges de Froidcourt, op. cit.

[3] See Grison, op. cit.

[4] See Philippe Maréchal: La Révolution dans la Haute Saône (Honoré Champion, Paris, 1903), who insists on the apocryphal nature of such stories which he ascribes to an (unnamed) popular author. I have also been assured by M. F. Le Bour' his-Kerbiziet, who has written so learnedly on Le bourreau et la guillotine en Bretagne (see La Nouvelle Revue de Bretagne, janvier-février, 1952, et seq.), that his researches revealed no reason to think that any blades other than the modern type were ever used.

same letter from Sanson to the Liège executioner, the former makes the situation clear once and for all. "As to the form of the axe", he writes, "it is not fixed and everyone makes it as he thinks best. . . ." [1]

Throughout its career, the guillotine has undergone a series of transformations. From the first it was apparent, for example, that a stouter scaffold was needed to bear the weight of a contraption notably more cumbersome than the present-day version; [2] then, too, there was a sequence of messily incomplete beheadings, and, on June 5th, 1792, the architect Giraud submitted a report [3] requested by Roederer which affirmed that the machine in which Schmidt had taken so ingenuous a pleasure, "although well conceived in itself, has not been perfected to the fullest possible extent"—an end, he pointed out, especially desirable to ensure "the public's peace of mind".

More specifically, Giraud noted that "the grooves, the tongues and the gudgeons are in wood; the first should be made of brass, the others of iron; the hooks to which are attached the cords holding up the *mouton* are only fixed with round-headed nails; they should be fixed with strong nuts and bolts.

"There is no step to the *bascule*, the straps are placed too low and are insufficiently solid and too open.

"Moreover, at least two *moutons* with their blades should be in reserve, for immediate replacement in the event of some accident occurring. . . ."

It was a comprehensive indictment, and there was a meaningful postscript: "*N.B.* A person for whom the undersigned architect can vouch offers to make this improved machine for the sum of 500 *livres*."

A bad business for Schmidt, that report. The blithe fellow

---

[1] A number of nineteenth-century prints show a curious scythe-shaped blade which may also be seen in the model guillotines at the Musée Carnavalet.

[2] See Taschereau, op. cit.

[3] Ibid.

had already taken out a patent in his own name on Dr Louis' creation; he had already constructed one or two additional machines for the provinces; there were then eighty-three Departments in France: each was to obtain—was fervently clamouring for—its own local guillotine; Schmidt could reasonably imagine that he was settled for life, due to touch an interesting and regular income disdained by the Glory of the *Académie chirurgical*. And behind his back, treacherously, this intrusive Giraud conspired with the *Procureur général syndic* to fleece him. The pitiful feud is glimpsed tantalisingly behind the obfuscating mass of administrative exchanges.

To the Minister of Finance on June 7th, 1792, M. Roederer addressed himself in a tone of shocked disappointment:

"In view of the enormous price originally demanded by M. Guidon . . . there was reason to think that M. Schmidt's propositions were disinterested and would give him no more than an honest return; but since then, having had reason to suspect that the machine should cost less by far than the sum asked by M. Schmidt, I have had a detailed examination made, and the result of an estimate drawn up . . . is that it is worth no more than 305 *livres*, 7 *sous*, 4 *deniers*, not including the leather bag, and 329 *livres* if this last is included. The same architect has drawn attention in a report to several defects; he has indicated the changes and additions necessary, and he only estimates 500 *livres* for a perfected machine. . . ."[1]

A little decent humility might still have saved Schmidt, but, on the contrary, he chose to display an inflexible rapacity. The 920 *livres* which he had charged for the original guillotine and its few successors could not be reduced below 824, he insisted, even on a contract to deliver the goods in quantity. Eight hundred and twenty-four *livres* (and on a large order, mind) for a machine worth 300! And an *improved* model offering for only 500! His calculations nourished M. Roederer's annoyance.

[1] Ibid.

And even before Giraud's report was handed in, M. Roederer had had reason to look austerely on Schmidt. Paris was being vexingly slow in distributing guillotines to the remoter districts; forbidden to execute their felons except in accordance with the new law and deprived of the means to do so, the provincial authorities were accumulating condemned men in excessive quantities. Always on the look-out for a good business opportunity, the alert Schmidt decided to seize the occasion to institute a black market in guillotines. Roederer cannot have been unaware of the letter received the previous May by the Ministry of Justice from the *Procureur syndic* of the Loire-Inférieure: [1]

"*M. le Ministre* is requested to arrange this despatch so that the law's vengeance shall not be delayed. An artist who does not give his name, but the same who built the machines for Paris and Versailles, has just offered his services. He proposes to supply one for this Department, but his offer involves a price which seems to me to be high. He speaks of 40 *louis*. . . ." [2]

In a letter dated June 30th, [3] M. Roederer again denounced the money-grubbing Schmidt (the only non-humanitarian in the affair) to the new Finance Minister, M. Beaulieu (that particular office was no more secure then than now). The latter, duly appalled at the revelations and anxious, no doubt, to show how conscientious a Finance Minister *could* be, required Tobias Schmidt to explain himself without delay.

Banking overmuch, perhaps, on his imagined indispensibility, Schmidt had his own ideas as to what constituted a delay. Not until somewhat more than a month later did he submit his apologia, and by that time he had still weightier accusations to answer. For on July 28th the implacable Roederer informed M. Beaulieu that "at the last execution, which

---

[1] See Le Bour'his-Kerbiziet, op. cit.
[2] Forty *louis* was equivalent to 960 *livres*.
[3] See Taschereau, op. cit.

took place in Paris this week, the neck of one of the victims
was not completely severed, and since the rope which is used
to haul up the *mouton* was withdrawn as soon as the *mouton*
was in position, it cannot be blamed for this accident, which
was probably due to the grooves being swollen. This draw-
back had been foreseen at the outset by the Sieur Schmidt
himself, who had at that time proposed to make the grooves
in brass; and only self-interest subsequently induced him to
avoid this expenditure. . . . The executioner residing at
Versailles has just this instant left the offices of this department, where he remarked that the blade of the machine in
the Seine-et-Oise was badly tempered, that it was already
chipped, and that he was afraid of some accident in connection
with the execution of five people which is due to take place
immediately. . . ." [1]

Poor, bedevilled Schmidt! That same day, the *Directoire* of
the Department of the Côte d'Or had sent him the following
baleful communication: [2]

"Monsieur: We have received the machine which you
despatched to us. The task confided to you could not have
been worse carried out. We could have built it much better
here for 300 *livres*. We are informing the Ministry of our
dissatisfaction."

Not that Schmidt himself was inactive in this warfare.
There was, after all, something involved; 83 machines at
824 *livres*: it was an affair. And spare parts. And replacements
of worn-out models. Those graceful inclinations which Dr
Louis had made in his direction when reporting on the Bicêtre
tests occurred to him; with easy effrontery, he called at
M. Roederer's own department, requesting a copy of Louis'
letter, "and he did not conceal", the *Procureur* exasperatedly
recorded, "that his aim was to take advantage of certain ex-
pressions in this letter when dealing with one of the National

[1] Ibid.
[2] See Clément-Janin: *Le Morimont de Dijon* (Chez Darantière, Dijon, 1889).

Assembly's committees, of whom he has apparently asked that the validity of his patent be maintained".[1]

By August 3rd, Schmidt had prepared his defence; the second of the Finance Ministers concerned had gone the way of all Finance Ministers, and it was to his successor, M. Le Roulx, that Schmidt now addressed himself:

"If the last execution carried out in Paris did not fulfil expectations, it is in no way due to any imperfection in the machine, which is without defect; it is because of a lack of precaution on the part of the executioner who was not careful to gather the two ends of the rope which supports the *mouton* and to hold them in such a way that they could not interfere with its movement. He failed to take this precaution and the rope was caught up between the blade and the cross-bar and prevented the *mouton* falling with its natural weight. . . ."[2]

An artful riposte, but quite useless; he cited the executioner's own brother as witness that the fault had been with that official, he referred with impressing mendacity to "my invention", he got off some telling allusions to Roederer's ignorance of the subtleties of carpentry and mechanics; but, even as he wrote, Giraud's friend (a M. Clairin, it turned out, in a small way of business over by the Théâtre-Français) had submitted his estimate,[3] calculated, one might say, at cut-throat prices and even providing that the machine should be delivered all ready in its coat of scarlet paint. There was no renewal of Schmidt's patent; the one person not only willing but eager to be recognised as the Widow's parent was ignominiously returned to his piano-harmonicas and diving-suits, supplanted by a commonplace Clairin.

Even the latter's shinily elaborated machine, however, was later found by the Revolutionaries to leave room for improvement. M. Mathiez[4] assures us that they were distressed by the

[1] See Taschereau, op. cit.   [2] See Pichon, op. cit.
[3] See Taschereau, op. cit.
[4] See A. Mathiez: *La Révolution Française* (Collection Armand Colin, Paris, 1938).

relatively lackadaisical pace at which it operated, although, one head off, it could be dealing with the next victim within sixty seconds. For the agents of the Terror, not Humanity, not even Reason formed the attraction of the guillotine, but its speed. Aristocrats, counter-revolutionaries, defeated generals, their own colleagues—there was such a lot to be done. The figures are wretched in comparison to the heroic achievements of later times; but the will was there, and the great slanted knife—so incontestably an improvement on earlier means— nonetheless fell too slowly for their taste.

Guyot de Fère [1] alleges that Danton himself called on Dr Guillotin in his retirement to design a three-bladed machine to aid the Republic and that the Doctor "*ne put supprimer l'élan de son indignation*"; and Croker [2] has an *on-dit* to the effect that a multiple-bladed contraption was actually built and intended for installation in the Palais de Justice, but, as with Fère, no details are given in support of the tale. Fleischmann [3] in turn quotes an anonymous pamphlet of 1803 which mentions "Seguy, Jean, surgeon, ex-municipal, juliéniste and blood-drinker" as "the tiger who ordered the building of the four-bladed guillotine" at Bordeaux. "Serious documents", says M. Fleischmann, "have never been forthcoming to support this affirmation", but he errs; such documentation does exist.

A Bordeaux historian [4] has submitted copious evidence that a four-bladed machine was indeed ordered, not, it is true, by the tigerish Seguy, but by Lacombe, president of the military commission in that city. Whether it ever functioned is un-certain, but it was unquestionably built, and at least one fascinating feature of the gargantuan scaffold on which it was mounted is known: there were trap-doors in the thing through

[1] See G.D.F., op. cit.
[2] See Croker, op. cit.
[3] See Fleischmann, op. cit.
[4] See G. Mirassem: *Chronique de Bordeaux: Ephémérides de la guillotine sous la Terreur à Bordeaux* (G. Maleville, Libourne, 1883).

which the corpses dropped down into waiting carts which, when filled, drove from beneath through a great doorway in one of the sides.

And even before the impatient citizenry at large began deploring their gadget's slowness, at least one prescient individual had busied himself with the problem of hurrying the process along. In 1793, a certain Guillot—perhaps inspired by the fact that his name was only a truncated version of the Master's—carried out experiments (and at Bicêtre, to preserve the unities) with a nine-bladed machine of his invention.[1] The trials were unsuccessful, and Guillot departs from the history as brusquely as he entered it.

But the transformations which were effectively carried out have been hardly less radical. Henry Sanson's improved method of bolting the blade to its weight [2] is perhaps not worth mentioning; but what stupendous unorthodoxy, what hectic unconventionality some of his successors displayed, Heindreicht and Roch especially. The former, it is true, resisted the proposal to fabricate an all-metal guillotine permanently mounted on wheels for greater mobility,[3] but, with a humanitarianism worthy of the high philosophic days of '89, he got rid of the scaffold, thus ending the ghastly ascent of ten steps which the condemned had hitherto been obliged to make. Flat on the ground, the guillotine was only half its old appalling self. And the benevolent creature painted the glittering blade a discreet, unnoticeable black, replaced the woodwork's symbolic scarlet with a reassuring dark brown.

His successor, M. Roch, was no less energetic in the cause of good executing. A point which had escaped Heindreicht's attention was that an iron grip was smashed down at the same time as the upper section of the *lunette*, penetrating the muscles of the neck and periodically causing a fracture of the

[1] See Paul Bru: *Histoire de Bicêtre* (Aux bureaux du progrès-Lescronier et Babé, Paris, 1890.)
[2] See *l'Illustration*, December 18th, 1909.
[3] Archives de la Seine: D3 U148.

occipital.[1] None of that sort of barbarism for M. Roch, and away it went. Then again (it is true that the conception was the prison chaplain's, the Abbé Crozes) he had carried Heindreicht's disguise of the awaiting blade still further. On September 1st, 1878, he informed the Abbé that "your wishes have been met, the request has been approved, and the excellent idea carried into effect",[2] that is, a wooden shield had been installed at the summit of the machine which should mask the knife from the sight of the approaching victim—a novelty suppressed by that sturdy traditionalist, M. Deibler, when in time he replaced the amiable Roch.

There were other refinements. A system of assembling the machine was developed which could be carried out in silence, whereas previously the fatal hammer-blows were audible throughout the night to the man in the condemned cell. Lastly—but this hardly mattered to the victim—Roch installed rubber shock-absorbers to put an end to the horrible double crash of the blade as it fell and rebounded. Well might he refer lovingly to his charge as "*le bijou*".[3]

By 1880 the guillotine had reached a stage of excellence which left room for few additional improvements. In three-quarters of a second the blade dropped from its high nest and sliced through the shrinking neck beneath, and better than that even today's model can barely manage.

[1] See Lacassagne, op. cit.
[2] See l'Abbé Moreau: *Souvenirs de la petite et de la grande Roquette* (Jules Rouffe et Cie, Paris, 1884).
[3] See Grison, *op. cit.*

CHAPTER SEVEN

IN the third week of April 1792, the Second Criminal Tribunal was still burdened with Nicolas-Jacques Pelletier, about whose already over-due execution it had begun to fuss at the Assembly early the previous month. On April 20th, his macabre honeymoon with Schmidt at its height of felicity, M. Roederer informed the *Commissaire du roi* attached to the Tribunal [1] that there would be no further delays: Pelletier might confidently ready himself for execution five days later on the place de Grève. [2] Guidon was occupied in building a scaffold stout enough to take the portentous shock of the guillotine's blade; Captain Fortin of the *Gendarmerie nationale* had been alerted; Lafayette, commanding the *Garde nationale*, had been warned that "the new method of carrying out the punishment of decapitation will certainly attract a considerable crowd to the Grève, and it will be as well to ensure that no damage is done to the machine". [3]

At half past three on the afternoon of April 25th, 1792, Pelletier, red-shirted as required by the law of his time, was led onto the scaffold. Before just such a large crowd as sapient M. Roederer had foreseen, Sanson operated the guillotine in dead earnest for the first time. Pelletier's head was whipped off without a hitch.

Press reaction was one of sober approbation, typified by the

[1] See Taschereau, op. cit.
[2] Now the place de l'Hôtel-de-Ville.
[3] See Taschereau, op. cit.

contented observation of one newspaper [1] that the new device "in no way stained any man's hand with the murder of his kind, and the speed with which it struck is more in accordance with the spirit of the law, which may often be severe but which should never be cruel".

But that large crowd, indifferent to or unaware of all the philanthropy around, was distinctly disappointed. The deliciously affrighting scenes of the old days were gone. One had to go back to 1626 for such an epic decapitation as that of the comte de Chalais, whose head was only hacked off at the twenty-ninth stroke of the sword and who was still living at the twentieth; [2] but even in modern times there had been some marvellously messy spectacles. But now . . . with this new-fangled apparatus: one hardly got a glimpse of anything. And the speed—that speed which had so rejoiced the *Commissaire du roi* at La Falaise, about which Dr Louis had been so whimsical, which the newspapers would next day applaud—it was sickening! The whole business was over before one had had a chance to enjoy it.

Officially, however, things could not have gone better. The provincial authorities demanded delivery of their guillotines more insistently than ever; Schmidt, unconscious of how brief was to be his tenure of office, went sunnily to work; Dr Guillotin was said to have exclaimed in ecstatic self-commendation that "the victim does not suffer at all, being conscious of nothing other than a slight chill on his neck", but, alas, the *mot* is only an elaboration of one of Dr Louis' witticisms, and it is not known whether Guillotin was even present to see Pelletier put the machine to the test.

It had all been a great success, but before very long the rejoicing officials—those who were left—would find that there were one or two unpleasantnesses connected with the new

[1] See *La Chronique de Paris*, April 26th, 1792.
[2] See Le Bour'his-Kerbiziet, op. cit. It is only fair to the profession to add that the executioner was a miserable amateur who had saved his own neck by consenting to slash the Count's.

method of execution, and those dogs lapping up their rich supper around the scaffold not the most distasteful. At Arras, for example, where Lebon's enthusiasm for republican principles necessitated a considerable number of executions, the *Conseil général* at its meeting on 2 ventôse, An II, peevishly noted that the guillotine was never properly cleaned after the day's work was done and that, in the summer especially, this made the immediate environs most disagreeable. Were good citizens, the Council demanded at a later session, to be poisoned by the stink of aristocrats' blood? Were the brutes to empest the air even after death? [1]

And there were similar annoyances in Paris. The guillotine had been shifted from the place de Grève to the place du Carroussel; to spare the delicate nerves of the deputies meeting in the near-by Tuileries, it had been shifted yet again; in July of 1794 it was lodged—one hoped for good and all —on the outskirts of the city, at the barrière du Trône. But no; on July 9th a police report noted that the hole which received the victims' blood was full and "emits a pestiferous odour of which the neighbouring inhabitants complain bitterly".[2]

All this was in the future, and on that April day no one could grudge the exhausted bureaucrats their moment of satisfaction: not for nine more months would an execution in the new style outdo the death of Pelletier in importance.

Under the fanged direction of Barère—"*l'Anacréon de la guillotine*"—the Assembly had listened to the evidence; Malesherbes had concluded his speech for the defence; too many deputies were showing signs of wishing to display a counter-revolutionary clemency, and "*la vertu*", said Robespierre, preparatory to putting a little pressure on these recusants "is always in the minority in this world"; by eight o'clock on the night of January 17th, 1793, 387 against 334 of the people's

[1] See Lenotre, op. cit.
[2] See C. A. Dauban: *Paris en 1794 et en 1795* (Plon, Paris, 1869).

representatives had submissively voted for the King's death.[1] Three days later, Charles-Henri Sanson, Executioner of the Criminal Sentences, was deep in final preparations to destroy the man who had named him to his post.

"I have just received the orders which you sent me", he wrote to the *Procureur général syndic*. "I will take all necessary measures to avoid any delay in what is called for. The carpenter has been advised about setting up the machine which will be erected at the point required.

"It is absolutely necessary that I should know how Louis will leave the Temple. Will he have a carriage or will he be in the ordinary vehicle used for executions of this kind? After the execution, what will happen to the body?

"Is it necessary that I or my assistants should be at the Temple at eight o'clock, as the order states?

"In the event that it is not I who bring him from the Temple, where exactly should I be waiting?

"None of these things being detailed in the order, it would be helpful if the *citoyen suppléant procureur-syndic* of the Department would be good enough to provide me as soon as possible with this information while I am occupied with giving the necessary orders so that everything is punctually executed [*sic*]".[2]

So many things to attend to, so much to think of; dying, Louis Capet was almost as much trouble as alive. There was the planning of the vast cortège which preceded his carriage; the stationing of troops along either side of the route between the Temple and the place de la Liberté;[3] Paris was in a state of siege.[4] How much of this display of republican might was necessary? The only incident during the King's journey to the scaffold was when four pitiful royalists called on the silent thousands about them to save His Majesty. Two of them were cut down where they stood; the others fled. The King

[1] See Madelin, op. cit.
[2] See Lenotre, op. cit.
[3] Now the place de la Concorde.
[4] See Madelin, op. cit.

seemed to have noticed nothing.[1] At twenty-two minutes past ten [2] on the morning of January 21st, 1793, the "huge Cyclopean axe", as Carlyle reverberatingly calls it, had fallen on its most august victim, and a hundred or so men and women were dancing about the scaffold and seeking to dip their fingers in the royal blood.[3]

Thanks to a journalist whose misrepresentation of the facts [4] provoked a reply, an account of the King's execution was forthcoming from the person most directly concerned after Louis himself.[5] "Here," wrote Sanson, "in accordance with my promise, is the exact truth of what took place at the execution of Louis Capet:

"Descending from the vehicle for the execution, he was told that he must remove his coat. He made some objection, saying that he could be executed as he was. On being given to understand that this was impossible, he himself helped remove his coat. He made the same objection when it was a question of tying his hands, which he himself held out when the person with him told him that it was a final sacrifice. Then he asked if the drums were still beaten. He was told that this was not known, which was the truth. He ascended the scaffold and wanted to move to the front of it, as if wishing to speak. But he was given to understand that this, too, was impossible. He then allowed himself to be led to the place where he was bound and whence he called very loudly: 'People, I die innocent!' Then, turning towards us, he said: 'Messieurs, I am innocent of everything with which I have been charged. I hope that my blood will cement the welfare of the French people!' Such, citizen, were his last and actual words.

"The sort of little argument which took place at the foot of the scaffold arose from his not thinking it necessary to remove

[1] See Fleischmann, op. cit.
[2] See Seligman, op. cit.
[3] An eye-witness account quoted by Lenotre, op. cit.
[4] See *Le Thermomètre du jour*, February 13th, 1793.
[5] Ibid., February 18th, 1793.

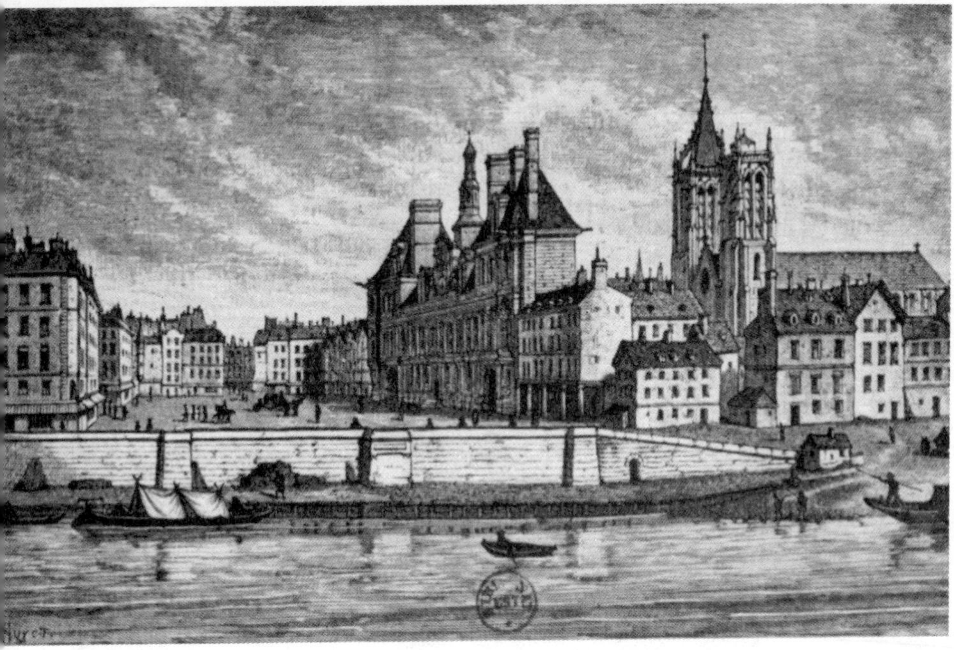

Bibliothèque nationale, Paris

The Place de Grève, scene of the first execution carried out by guillotine

PLATE VII

The execution of Louis XVI. From a contemporary print

Bibliothèque nationale, Paris

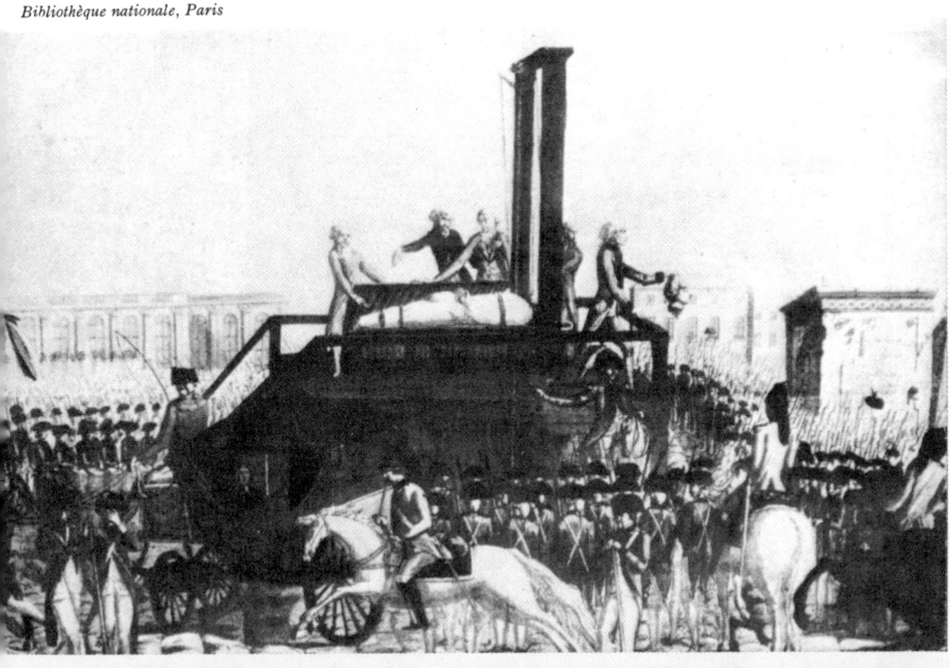

Feldhaus-Archiv, Wilhelmshaven

The guillotine as imagined by a German artist

PLATE VIII

his coat or to have his hands tied. He also suggested that he himself should cut his hair.

"And, to be quite truthful, he bore it all with a sang-froid and a firmness which astonished us. I am very sure that he derived this firmness from those religious principles with which no one could seem more endowed than he. . . ."

The tribute was a generous one, but hardly demanding as much courage of so indispensable a public servant as has been represented; nor does Sanson's little reportage justify the continuing ingenuous belief in all the legends about the man's alleged monarchist tendencies and his anguished remorse over his own act of regicide. There is no corroboration for the stories of such romantic melancholy; nor is it true that he did yearly penance on the site of the execution; nor, on the other hand, that he died of lèse-majesté a few days after the King's death; nor that he paid for masses to be said for the repose of his victim's soul—this last a piece of sentimental fiction by Balzac.[1] The headsman's solitary service to the King he killed was a negative one—neither he nor his assistants took any part in the sale of locks of Louis' hair to republican souvenir-hunters.[2]

The execution of Louis XVI has tended to obscure subsequent guillotinings of equal, although less epic, interest. And the Queen, apologising to Sanson when she accidentally trod on his foot; the Dubarry, pleading with the executioner (as if he, poor brute, could arrest the process) for a few seconds' stay; the long procession of unnamed aristocrats, derisively acknowledging the execration of the crowd, laughing among themselves as they stood on the scaffold waiting their turn, taking urbane leave of each other when Sanson beckoned [3]—

[1] See Honoré de Balzac: *Un Episode sous la Terreur* (*Scènes de la vie Politique*, Hachette, Paris, 1853).

[2] See *Le Thermomètre du jour*, January 29th, 1793.

[3] There is massive contemporary documentation to indicate that most of the aristocrats did behave with just such extraordinary panache. It has even been suggested that their apparent indifference alone enabled the public to endure the incessant executions.

these have overshadowed occasions well worth attention, perhaps even more indicative of the thoroughgoing enthusiasm which characterised the Terror.

It has not been possible to confirm the legend that a dog which had been taught to howl whenever it heard the word "republican" was guillotined along with its master; but there is nothing inherently improbable in the story. It is no more ridiculous, for instance, than the decapitation of Valazé. He was guilty of a crime still graver than that of howling at a word; he had picked the wrong side. Arrested as a Girondin, he and his accomplices were (what else?) condemned to death, but Valazé—and it was additional confirmation of his deviationism—would not accept the idea of dying at the hands of the enemy. On the eve of his execution, he committed suicide. He was sadly ingenuous in thinking that it was as easy as that to deprive the Government of its fun; his corpse was bundled into the cart which was to take his associates to the scaffold; and the dead Valazé was triumphantly decapitated with the rest.[1]

And if a dog, if a corpse, why not children? The omission was rectified at Nantes on December 17th, 1793, when two children of fourteen and two of thirteen were included among the twenty-four individuals selected for summary execution that day.[2]

Why limit the treatment to members of the canine or human race at all? The rationalists of the Revolution reflected briefly; then wooden figures of the saints were carted from the churches and guillotined;[3] Lejeune chose the birds for his dinner-table and had them guillotined;[4] to celebrate the anniversary of the King's death, Albitte assembled effigies of reigning monarchs and had them guillotined;[5] the Breton

[1] See Madelin, op. cit.
[2] See Biré, op. cit.
[3] See Jules Michelet: *Histoire de la Révolution française* (C. Marpon & E. Flammarion, Paris, 1868).
[4] See *Le Moniteur*, 18 prairial, An III.
[5] See Fleischmann, op. cit.

schoolteacher, Guillaume Kerhouant, built dummies of notorious *émigrés* and, for the instruction of his pupils, had them guillotined.[1] The machine provided endlessly varied entertainment.

But the carrying out of mere criminal sentences, too, has often been accompanied by circumstances of interest: sometimes a remarkable last word ("*N'avouez jamais!*"), sometimes a glimmer of almost aristocratic panache (waving aside the proffered glass of rum with the comment "I lose all sense of direction when I'm drunk"), sometimes a stupendous revelation of the murderer's mind (Moyse, killer of his own son, greeting the executioner's arrival with the outraged cry: "What! Would you execute the father of a family?"). Sometimes—perhaps every time—a bizarre *mise-en-scène*, as in the case of Troppmann.[2]

That was an occasion! Nothing was left undone to ensure that it all went with a swing. Like crowds outside the Opera on a gala night, the mob waited on the place de la Roquette in the aching cold to see the privileged arrive and pass through the doors. And within the prison, what animation! what good-fellowship! In the courtyard coffee was served to the assembled troops; the prison pharmacist entertained fifteen acquaintances to truffled turkey; and in the Director's apartment the servants moved quietly around under the brilliant chandeliers offering sandwiches, *pâté de foie gras*, cold chicken, tea, punch, and wine. The guests were unanimous that it was one of the Director's most successful receptions.

And such guests! It was rather a literary affair, but with no flavour of Grub Street about it. Maxime Du Camp was there and had brought along the distinguished Muscovite Turgeneff,[3] who had already had the deliciously disturbing thrill of being

[1] See Albert Macé: *Un Instituteur en l'An II* (V. Forest et E. Grimaud, Nantes, 1884).

[2] See l'Abbé Moreau, op. cit.

[3] See Ivan Turgeneff: *Devant la guillotine* (Flammarion, Paris, 1892). This work appears never to have been translated into English.

mistaken for the executioner; Victorien Sardou turned up
punctually; no end of celebrities.

Outside, Heindreicht and his men were erecting the guillotine. One or two of the Director's friends strolled out to watch
the work; caught up in the prevailing mood of geniality, the
bourreau invited them to come onto the platform and inspect
things at close quarters; the guests were charmed; affable
Heindreicht explained the mechanism, pointed out little
features with modest pride; M. Sardou was among the group:
in a final spasm of hilarity, he insisted on being placed on the
bascule. The headsman entered into the spirit of the thing,
seized the humorous author, pushed him onto the plank. One
of the bales of straw used to test the blade before each execution
was laid where his neck should have been. The blade flashed
down, sliced through the straw an inch or so away from M.
Sardou's head. It was irresistible! Everyone was in splendid
humour by the time Troppmann was led out past the cordon
of troops, their swords lifted in the traditional salute, to replace
the man of letters.

For Troppmann the moment was somewhat more serious;
but he, too, all involuntarily, made a contribution to the
special atmosphere of the event, and one which the assembled
literary men noted with trepidant relish. The murderer had
fought against fulfilment of his ignoble destiny ever since his
arrest: he had demanded a retrial and been refused; he had
appealed for the Emperor's clemency and, when that was
withheld, had sought to defer his rendezvous with Heindreicht by suggesting that he might at last reveal the names of
his non-existent accomplices. None of it worked; his meeting
with the *bourreau* grew imminent; in the cloud-cuckoo-land
of his helplessness, he offered the prison pharmacist (now helping friends to truffled turkey) a bribe to bring him poison,
tried the same bribe on an inspector of the Sûreté, hinted to a
visiting priest that the latter might lend his soutane to facilitate
an escape. Now, thrust between the uprights, his neck encircled

by the *lunette*, that maniacal determination not to die at the hands of the executioner dictated a final gesture of revolt. He arched his body in a spasm of denial and succeeded in drawing back his head. The assistant executioner [1] made a move to grab his hair and pull him into position. In the fraction of a second the blade crashed down, Troppmann managed to make one last ludicrous assault on society. He stretched his neck obligingly forward and sank his teeth deep in the assistant's hand.

[1] To avoid any risk of excessive mutilation, this functionary is charged to ensure that the condemned man does not draw his head into his shoulders. He arranges this by pulling the victim forward by the hair or—should baldness make this impracticable—by the ears. Because of his concern with settling the patient in position, he is known in criminal slang as "the photographer".

CHAPTER EIGHT

THERE is an execution as awe-inspiring as any visited on a king or a corpse or a dog or a Troppmann: the execution which took place yesterday or which will take place tomorrow —the commonplace, unnoticed removal from existence of the anonymous murderer.

At the execution of Lally, says Mme Du Deffand,[1] the audience clapped hands at the progress of the entertainment. It was an old tradition and it persisted long after. When Allorto and Sellier were guillotined in 1889, the crowd demonstrated the same child-like enthusiasm. The Paris Exhibition was at its height—there were endless amusements offering—but this one momentarily did bigger business than even M. Eiffel's fabulous tower. Thomas Cook & Co. included it in their list of attractions and provided seven large horse-buses to take the tourists along. The thing was programmed for an early hour—attendance was quite as fatiguing as any of the conducted tours of Montmartre— but each of the forty seats in each of the seven buses was filled.[2]

Executions are no longer public in France. For a long time they were only so in principle anyway, since they took place at dawn and the crowds were held well back by a cordon of police. But in 1939 Weidmann was guillotined outside the prison at Versailles; it was the culmination of a genuine *cause célèbre* and there were numerous onlookers; conditions at Versailles were ideal for them and their Dickensian relish was

[1] See *Lettres de la Marquise Du Deffand* (Firmin Didot, Paris, 1864).
[2] See Graven, op. cit.

altogether too much for prissy Authority. Throughout the night, it is said, the condemned man could hear the jovial mob whiling away the time which must elapse before things got under way. They perched on window-ledges and in the branches of trees; all apartments with a view on the place had been rented at heroic prices long before; buskers diverted the gathering until such time as M. Desfourneaux and his assistants arrived to begin the curtain-raiser—the punctilious setting-up of their machine. Quantities of wine were exuberantly drunk, songs were sung, jests exchanged.

Not that it gave pain to the bear, but that it gave pleasure to the spectators. . . . The Decree of June 24th, 1939, limited these occasions henceforward to the melancholy confines of a prison-yard, and the new Article 26 of the *Code Pénal* reserved all the fun to nine officials: the presiding judge of the Assizes or, failing him, a magistrate nominated by the *premier président*; an officer of the Public Prosecutor's Office designated by the *Procureur général*; a judge of the Tribunal in the district where the execution is to take place; the clerk of the Court of the Assizes or, failing him, a clerk of the Court from the Tribunal in the district where the execution is to take place; defence counsel for the condemned man; a minister of religion; the Director of the penitentiary; the *commissaire* of police and, if required, such members of the police force as may be ordered by the *Procureur général* or the *Procureur de la République*; the prison doctor or, failing him, a doctor designated by the *Procureur général* or the *Procureur de la République*.

Until the last moment the condemned man can hope to avoid an appearance before this select audience: he learns that his appeal for clemency has been rejected only when he is awakened by the officials charged to hand him over to the executioner. Nightly, he must go to sleep wondering if the guillotine is even then being silently mounted in the courtyard for the removal of his head a few hours later. Only on Saturday nights and the nights preceding religious or national fête days

can he sleep without apprehension, knowing that Article 25
of the *Code Pénal* prohibits the carrying out of death sentences
on those days. If a woman and pregnant, the condemned
prisoner need have no uneasiness until after the birth of the
child.[1] If a parricide, he need no longer anticipate that he will
be "led to the place of execution barefooted, clad in a shirt, and
having his head covered with a black veil" although the law
still provides for this refinement [2] and its application is said to
have continued at least until 1929.[3]

French courts condemn a man to death matter-of-factly,
with none of the infernal theatricals which are put on elsewhere. The presiding judge announces *"Peine de mort"* in a
voice which declines to recognise it as either a triumph of
society or a regrettable necessity. It is a fact. The prisoner is
returned to his prison, in the *Quartier de Haute Surveillance*.

The law provides that "unless the number of condemned
prisoners in the establishment makes it absolutely necessary to
group them", each shall have his private cell. A window gives
on to the adjoining room; through it, warders watch the promised victim night and day; watched and watcher talk together
and the topic rarely changes: What are the chances that the
Cour de Cassation will quash the sentence on a technicality?
That the *Conseil Supérieur de la Magistrature* will discover some
extenuating circumstances? That—last hope of all—the President of the Republic will himself decide in favour of a
reprieve? The warder answers reassuringly, confidently, and
never more so than on that night when a colleague has whis-
pered in his ear, *"C'est pour demain"*.[4]

---

[1] Although the law does not distinguish between men and women, in fact
the latter are always reprieved. This has been the tradition for many years,
except during Marshal Pétain's reign and in the immediate post-war period.
[2] Article 13 of the *Code Pénal*.
[3] See B. and P. Dabat: *Souvenirs d'un Directeur de Prison* (Editions et publications contemporaines, Paris, 1929).
[4] For an account of the relations between warder and prisoner, see the
recollections of Maurice Aubenas quoted by Henri Danjou in the series *Nous
ne sommes pas tous des Assassins* (*France-Soir*, August 1st, 1952, *et seq.*).

Each tic and gesture of the prisoner's remaining days is covered by regulation. He is no longer subjected to the strait-jacket which was once obligatory for all in his circumstances; he is no longer shackled with leg-irons; [1] he may smoke all he wishes, buy himself gastronomic dainties from the prison canteen, receive visits in his cell from the chaplain, his barrister, the prison's social worker. It may continue for a long time.

It may come abruptly to an end. The President has made up his mind; innumerable functionaries set to work; Monsieur de Paris receives a communication:

"In the name of the Law:

"M. the Executioner of the High Works is hereby ordered to take possession of the individual named......condemned to the punishment of death by the Assizes Court of......on ......and to proceed with his execution within the confines of the prison of......on......at the legally-established hour of daybreak."

Less formally (see Plate XII) the executioner convokes his assistants—his "*valets*", in the light-hearted slang of the profession—to the meeting.

As far as Paris is concerned, that spoil-sport Decree of June 24th, 1939, means that all contemporary impositions of Dr Guillotin's principles must take place in the yard of the Santé prison; and in a hangar opening onto the *Cour d'Honneur* of that establishment, the two existing guillotines—once the personal charge of the headsman and kept by him in a dingy, unnumbered little house near the Prison de la Roquette—are now lodged, ready to hand.

There is not really very much to the guillotine: a great wooden cross weighing some 250 pounds to serve as base, the uprights, the cross-bar at the top, the two pieces of the *lunette* (the upper section shifting in grooves cut parallel with those

---

[1] A reform due to the film of André Cayatte and Charles Spaak, *Nous sommes tous des Assassins*.

which guide the blade), the wide wooden bench on which the victim lies, a rope running over the single pulley on top of the cross-bar and attached at one end to the knife. All the rest are accessories: a little bucket for the head, a zinc-lined basket for the body, a shield like the one used by oxy-acetylene welders which is to protect the "photographer" from "the spurt of blood which the heart, caught short, unaware that it is now only serving a corpse, continues to force through the arteries of the severed neck. . . ."[1]

Good workmen, in their workmen's blue overalls, the assistant executioners assemble the guillotine in the prison yard. With a spirit-level, they check its position, push wedges beneath the base to bring the thing to exact vertical. The chief executioner tests the fall of the blade. It is all ready.

A little before dawn, two warders approach the condemned man's cell. They are in stockinged feet: nothing must disturb the prisoner's last few seconds' sleep. Suddenly they open the door, cross rapidly to the condemned man and seize him before he has had time to realise that this is no mere continuation of his dreams. The chaplain, the officials who have waited outside in the corridor, enter the cell. The prison Director speaks the traditional words: "Your appeal has been rejected. Be brave."

There is no hurry. The victim may smoke a final cigarette, drink a final glass of rum, write a letter, receive—if he wants it—such consolation as the chaplain can provide. He is dressed in the clothes he was wearing when he returned from the court to the condemned cell. Once or twice it has happened that the warder collecting the garments from the storeroom has included the man's hat.

From the cell he is conducted to the records office. The *bourreau's* assistants have laid out on a table the simple articles needed for the "*toilette*", the final preparation of the victim. With a pair of shears they cut his hair from the back of the neck and hack away the upper part of his shirt: there must

[1] See Georges Arnaud: *Prisons 53* (Julliard, Paris, 1953).

be no risk of anything obstructing the fall of the blade. Cords have already been cut to appropriate lengths; just before they are used to tie the prisoner's wrists and ankles, there is a necessary formality to be undergone. His record-sheet is produced; he signs it; underneath, the Director writes, "Handed over to M. the Executioner for carrying out of the sentence". Monsieur de Paris initials the document. Everything is now in order. The man no longer belongs to the prison authorities. He is the property of the executioner.

It is only a short distance to the machine. With the gesture of gentlemen helping an old lady across the street, two of the assistant executioners take the condemned man by the arms. Hobbled by the cords, he can only walk with short steps. He is brought, with this insane obligatory courtesy, to the guillotine. The assistants thrust him sharply against the *bascule*. It tips him into position. The *lunette* closes around his neck. Monsieur de Paris presses the lever. The jaws of the grab open. The knife falls. The head drops into the bucket, the body is tipped sideways into the long coffin-shaped basket. Society can breathe again.

CHAPTER NINE

PROPOSED, adopted, built and perfected (all those concerned tirelessly insisted) solely from high philanthropic motives, the guillotine has nevertheless been the subject of speculative examination almost from the beginning of its existence. Was decapitation really so great an advance on burning, disembowelling, strangling and such other ingenuities as had, from time to time, been thought up? The philanthropists wondered.

Even before the guillotine itself went into action, a thoughtful medical man [1] had considered the merits and demerits of head-chopping and had finally expressed his belief that "the severed head still retains the faculty of feeling and thinking during several seconds". When the guillotine did appear, public interest in decapitation was marvellously aroused and, in addition to the pronouncements of science, a popular mythology rapidly grew up which culminated in Villier de l'Isle Adam's fantastical account of experiments allegedly carried out by Dr Velpeau on the head of the murderer La Pommerais.[2]

The guillotine was, incontestably, an improvement on the

[1] See Pierre Gautier: *La tête d'un décollé, conserve-t-elle, plusieurs instants après sa décollation du tronc, la faculté de sentir?* (Paris, 1776).

[2] See Villiers de l'Isle Adam: *Le Secret de l'Echafaud* (*L'Amour suprême*, Maurice de Brunhoff, Paris, 1886). Villier's use of actual individuals as characters (La Pommerais was executed on June 9th, 1864, on the place de la Roquette, and Dr Velpeau frequently attended executions, although not, as it happened, this one) resulted in his story being widely accepted as fact, and even offered as such up to the present day. The Abbé Crozes, however, chaplain at La Roquette, has given his assurance that no experiment of any sort was conducted. (See l'Abbé Moreau, op. cit.).

technique of even the handiest swordsman, but that it was wholly in accordance with the generous spirit of the age . . . a doubt persisted. Already in 1793 there was a story circulating —guaranteed, unarguable, sworn to by personal acquaintances of friends of eye-witnesses—in connection with the execution of Charlotte Corday. Severed, her head was ceremoniously held up for the enjoyment of the mob; in an excess of republican ardour the assistant executioner, François le Gros, struck one cheek with his open hand. Assembled to see the People's Friend revenged, the people even so cried out in disgust; the Conventionnel, Sergeant-Marceau, demanded that this unauthorised sadism be denounced by the *Tribunal révolutionnaire*; [1] Prudhomme spoke [2] of "infamy" and "atrocity"; and Mlle Corday, it would seem, was herself no less offended, for (a sober authority has recorded) "long after its separation from the body, Charlotte Corday's head showed in its countenance the most unequivocal signs of indignation. . . . Both cheeks reddened perceptibly. . . . It cannot be claimed that this flush resulted from the blow itself, for the cheeks of corpses may be struck this way in vain; they never colour: moreover, this blow was only struck on one cheek, and it was remarked that the other cheek also coloured. . . ."[3]

Such a topic might almost have been invented for the exercise of Teutonic ratiocination, and, on *18 brumaire, l'an IV de la République une et indivisible*, a letter of effortless finality, from the German anatomist S. T. Soemmering to his colleague and compatriot Oesler, appeared in a Paris daily.[4] "It is easy", announced the sage, "to demonstrate to anyone with the slightest knowledge of our bodies' construction and vital forces, that feeling is not entirely destroyed by this form of

---

[1] See Cabanès, op. cit.

[2] See Prudhomme: *Les Révolutions de Paris*, No. 198, du 20 au 27 avril, 1793.

[3] See Pierre Sue: *Opinion du Cen. Sue, professeur de médecine et de botanique, sur le supplice de la guillotine*. (No publisher, no date.)

[4] See *Le Moniteur*, November 9th, 1795.

capital punishment. What we are putting forward is founded
not on suppositions and hypotheses, but on facts: Those who
are convinced: 1. That the seat of feeling and its perception is
in the brain; 2. That the workings of this consciousness of
feeling can continue whether the circulation of the blood
through the brain be suspended or feeble or partial; need no
more than these accepted facts to draw the conclusion that the
guillotine must be a horrible form of death.

"*Feeling*", proclaimed Soemmering in a flurry of italics,
"the *personality*, the *ego* remain alive for some time in the head
which has been separated from the victim's body, and there
remains the *post-operative pain*" (if one may so translate the
writer's "*arrière-douleur*") "from which the neck suffers. . . ."

That *deus ex consulting-room* manner of his did not blind
Professor Soemmering to the possibility that there were
uninstructed individuals who might hesitate to accept his
dicta. "For the benefit of those who, lacking an exact knowledge of its source, may find this truth less evident, let us",
he suggested kindlily, "develop it", and develop it he did,
interspersing his thesis with fetching anecdotes of severed
heads that ground their teeth, bit each other as they lay side by
side in the basket, grimaced and soundlessly snarled. "If the
air still circulated through the vocal organs," said Soemmering
firmly, "*these heads would speak*. . . ." The only thing unknown apparently to the Professor was what they would say.

"You have yourself witnessed", he reminded his corre-
spondent in a vehement peroration, "the horrible convulsions
of the guillotined person; you have seen the frightful apparatus, the atrocious bonds, the hideous hair-cut, the indecent
nakedness, the blood which covers the mutilated body and the
execrable headsman; you have seen all the barbarous horrors
of this butchery, all those infamies which dishonour humanity
and which accompany this cruel and painful type of execution.
Such abominable spectacles ought not to take place among
savages: and yet they are republicans who provide them and

attend them." Three exclamation marks were needed to emphasise the anatomist's emotion.

Wedekind, Le Pelletier, Sedillot—half the medical profession came out in rebuttal of Soemmering's argument; but it was Sedillot [1] who adopted the unkindest method of opposing his colleague. In allusion to the anatomist's correlation of feeling with nervous spasms, he pointed out that "one is a sensation which affects the soul, while the other . . . can exist independently of any feeling", but that was simply in order to clear the ground. Where he was really a little malicious was in citing Soemmering himself as saying that "the faculty of perception, or the consciousness of feelings, ceases in ordinary sleep", for, argued Sedillot nastily, "if awareness of feeling ceases in ordinary sleep . . . how can anyone imagine that in death itself, after a punishment which has obliterated all the vital functions at one stroke—how can anyone imagine that in the head separated from the body there could remain this awareness of feeling, this appreciation of pain, which is necessarily the product of the combined action of the vital functions in their most perfect and unified state?"

That appeal to his own authority must have touched Professor Soemmering since he seems thereafter to have withdrawn from the whole debate; but similar solemn zanies (for all their worthiness) continued to emerge intermittently from then on, each time provoking their more orthodox confrères to object that so much as to think of consciousness surviving after decapitation was to blaspheme the medical gods.

Not until something like a century after Soemmering's outburst does the squabble produce any documentation of genuine interest. In the year 1879, a twenty-three-year-old peasant, Théotime Prunier, murdered an elderly woman. He raped the corpse and threw it into the river, subsequently

---

[1] See Dr Jean Sedillot: *Réflexions historiques et physiologiques sur le supplice de la guillotine* (Debray, Paris, An IV). In the same connection, see René-Georges Gastellier: *Que penser enfin du supplice de la guillotine?* (Chez les marchands de nouveautés, Paris, 1795).

returning in order to drag it from the water and again violate it. He was arrested the following morning (being woken from an untroubled sleep), tried and condemned to death. His execution was fixed for November 13th.

Even the necrophilous element hardly transforms his crime into anything of particular originality; but the Drs E. Decaisne, G. Decaisne and Evrard contemplated the killer's sturdy physique and brutish stolidity with a special interest. Dr E. Decaisne especially had long concerned himself with the problem of whether decapitation permitted some survival of consciousness. Prunier was an admirable specimen for experimentation.[1]

The murderer was awakened in Beauvais prison on the due date and informed that he was to die. He accepted the advice with seeming calm, although his face grew somewhat pale and his pulse (thoughtfully taken by the careful doctor) quickened to eighty-four per minute. He shook hands with his warders, thanked the chaplain with proper respect, and was delivered over to the executioner. He was guillotined at precisely 7 a.m.

By five past seven, the doctors, excited as children, were in possession of both body and head. They noted with satisfaction that there were no bloodstains in the region of the lips and ears, indicating that there had been no convulsive movements of the head after its severance. For the rest, "the eyes were closed. If one half-opened the lids, the eyeball was seen to be fixed and sunken. The pupils were equal in size and somewhat dilated. The face was pale, dull, completely bloodless and wore a look of astonishment. . . ." In the chill air (the experiment took place in the middle of the cemetery in the open) the earnest enquirers set to work.

Placing his mouth as near as possible to Prunier's ear, one of them called him loudly and repeatedly by name but without occasioning any movement of the face or eyes which

[1] See Charles Desmaze: *Histoire de la médecine légale en France* (G. Charpentier, Paris, 1880).

might have betokened perception. A sequence of teasings followed: Prunier was pinched on the cheek, a brush steeped in concentrated ammonia was inserted in his nostrils, a pencil of silver nitrate was drawn over the conjunctiva, a lighted candle held so close to the wide-open eyes that the flame touched the eyeball. No slightest movement or contraction took place: it was all distinctly disappointing.

In the following year, Dr Dassy de Lignières conducted a rather different experiment.[1] Three hours after the execution of the murderer Menesclou (on September 7th, 1880) the investigator began to pump blood from a living dog[2] into the criminal's head, and this time the results were . . . stimulating. The transfusion had only just begun when Menesclou's face reddened, his lips swelled and coloured visibly, his features took on a sharpened form. "It is no longer the livid and flaccid mask of a minute before", Dr de Lignières recorded, breaking into the historic present in his remembered excitement; "this head is about to speak, for it has just become animated by the beating of a heart."

There were still greater excitements in store. As the transfusion proceeded, suddenly, unmistakably, for a period of two seconds, the lips stammered silently, the eyelids twitched and worked, the whole face wakened into an expression of shocked amazement.

"I affirm", wrote the doctor, "that during two seconds the brain thought. . . ." Himself fully persuaded of the validity of his experience, Dr Dassy de Lignières did not hesitate to take up an unequivocal stand: "There is no worse torture than decapitation with the machine invented by that sensitive and humanitarian deputy, Dr Guillotin. . . . When the knife has done its work, has fallen with that sinister noise which you know, when the head has rolled into the sawdust . . . *this*

[1] See *Le Matin*, March 3rd, 1907.
[2] Anti-vivisectionists will be relieved to learn thàt the animal suffered no ill-effects from the incident.

head, separated from its body, hears the voices of the crowd. The decapitated victim feels himself dying in the basket. He sees the guillotine and the light of day."

Dr Lignières' researches notwithstanding, and despite Dr Decaisne, the question still remained as to whether the head of a guillotined man, without the gratuitous sustenance of dog's blood, did—or, at any rate, might—retain a momentary consciousness. For, as he himself allowed, Decaisne's experiment lacked certain important conditions: continued consciousness was possible, if at all, only for a matter of seconds—a minute at most—immediately after decapitation, and the scientists of Beauvais had not even begun their performance until five minutes after the head tumbled into the basket. Again, no attempt had been made to check the abundant hæmorrhage, and this was of prime importance.

Twenty-five years later, Dr Beaurieux, in perfect circumstances, went to work on the head of Languille, guillotined at 5.30 a.m. on June 28th, 1905. Dr Beaurieux' recital,[1] more remarkable than Lignières' and flatly contradicting Decaisne's, is so fascinating that it must be quoted at length:

"I consider it essential for you to know that Languille displayed an extraordinary sang-froid and even courage from the moment when he was told that his last hour had come until the moment when he walked firmly to the scaffold. It may well be, in fact, that the conditions for observation, and consequently the phenomena, differ greatly according to whether the condemned persons retain all their sang-froid and are fully in control of themselves, or whether they are in such a state of physical and mental prostration that they have to be carried to the place of execution and are already half-dead and as though paralysed by the appalling anguish of the fatal instant.

"The head fell on the severed surface of the neck and I did not therefore have to take it up in my hands, as all the newspapers have vied with each other in repeating; I was not

[1] See *Archives d'Anthropologie criminelle*, t. XX, 1905.

obliged even to touch it in order to set it upright. Chance served me well for the observation which I wished to make.

"Here, then, is what I was able to note immediately after the decapitation: the eyelids and lips of the guillotined man worked in irregularly rhythmic contractions for about five or six seconds. This phenomenon has been remarked by all those finding themselves in the same conditions as myself for observing what happens after the severing of the neck. . . .

"I waited for several seconds. The spasmodic movements ceased. The face relaxed, the lids half closed on the eyeballs, leaving only the white of the conjunctiva visible, exactly as in the dying whom we have occasion to see every day in the exercise of our profession or as in those just dead. It was then that I called in a strong, sharp voice: 'Languille!' I then saw the eyelids slowly lift up, without any spasmodic contraction —I insist advisedly on this peculiarity—but with an even movement, quite distinct and normal, such as happens in everyday life, with people awakened or torn from their thoughts. Next Languille's eyes very definitely fixed themselves on mine and the pupils focused themselves. I was not, then, dealing with the sort of vague dull look without any expression that can be observed any day in dying people to whom one speaks: I was dealing with undeniably living eyes which were looking at me.

"After several seconds, the eyelids closed again, slowly and evenly, and the head took on the same appearance as it had had before I called out.

"It was at that point that I called out again and, once more, without any spasm, slowly, the eyelids lifted and undeniably living eyes fixed themselves on mine with perhaps even more penetration than the first time. Then there was a further closing of the eyelids, but now less complete. I attempted the effect of a third call; there was no further movement—and the eyes took on the glazed look which they have in the dead. .

"I have just recounted to you with rigorous exactness what

I was able to observe. The whole thing had lasted twenty-five to thirty seconds.

"Dr Pettigand, who was present at the execution of an Annamite whose head likewise fell on the severed section (which, he says, reduced the hæmorrhage to a minimum), also saw the eyes of the decapitated man fix themselves on his and follow him round in a circular movement. The victim's regard even pursued him when he changed direction in an effort to escape from it. . . ."

The conclusions to which Dr Beaurieux was driven were, as might be expected, not dissimilar to those reached by Professor Soemmering more than a century before, and he was able to refer to three exceedingly distinguished colleagues [1] who, like himself, "unhesitatingly accept the idea of a superior reflex which has its starting-point in the excitation of the auditory nerves and which culminates, through the medium of the intrabulbar nuclei, in the excitation of the visual nerves. For such a reflex to occur, it must be admitted that the brain as a whole retains a survival of all its elements. . . . An undeniable fact remains: the sense of hearing and the sense of sight survived during twenty-five to thirty seconds after decapitation. Now, I wonder why, if the survival of the lower brain is unreservedly admitted, the survival of the upper brain—that is, consciousness—is categorically denied. I certainly have no wish", the doctor added piously, "to create an imaginative novel when dealing with a question of physiology. Nonetheless, if the survival of the intrabulbar nuclea is admitted, you will surely allow that the cortex may survive, and that there is no reason to deny the possibility of this survival. Conscious perception cannot be revealed to us except by the subject himself. That is why the problem, scientifically speaking, is insoluble. But it remains nonetheless true that the hypothesis of conscious perception cannot be rejected *a priori* and deserves to be discussed. . . ."

[1] Drs Hartmann, Langlois and Manouvrier.

It has been, it will be discussed; and the practical investigation of the problem still goes on. The most recent experimenters are Dr Piedelièvre and Dr Fournier,[1] who have concluded that "death is not instantaneous. . . . Every vital element survives decapitation. . . . (It is) a savage vivisection followed by a premature burial. . . ."

Most present-day physiologists, secure in their merely theoretical acquaintance with the issue, display a proper reserve towards so bizarre and nightmarish a notion as that of a head, separated from its trunk, contemplating its own horrendous state. Even so, they are unwilling to affirm flatly that it is out of the question. The possibility grimaces at us still.

[1] See *Justice sans bourreau*, June 1956.

CHAPTER TEN

"*Sunt irregulares ex defectu*", on the authority of Canon Law, "*qui munus carnificis susceperint voluntarii ac immediati ministri in exsecutione capitalis sententiae.*" [1] The Roman Catholic Church thus realistically incorporates in its code something of the instinctive aversion which is invariably felt for the public executioner.

"Who then is this incomprehensible being", asks de Maistre,[2] "who has preferred above all the pleasant, lucrative, honest and even honourable activities so abundantly available to human strength or skill that of torturing or putting to death his own kind? . . . The authorities have no sooner allocated him his dwelling-place, he has no sooner entered into possession of it than the other habitations recoil until they are no longer in sight of his. It is amidst this solitude, this sort of emptiness which encloses him that he lives alone with his female and his young; they acquaint him with the human voice; without them, he would know nothing but the sound of moaning. . . . A grisly signal is given; some abject agent of the law comes to his door and knocks and warns him that he is needed; he sets forth; he comes to a public place covered with an eager and palpitating crowd. A prisoner, a parricide, a blasphemer is thrown to him; he seizes him, stretches him out, binds him to a horizontal cross; he raises his arm; a

[1] See *Epitome Iuris Canonici*, t. II (H. Dessain, Rome, 1934).
[2] See Joseph de Maistre: *Les Soirées de Saint-Pétersbourg, ou Entretiens sur le gouvernement temporel de la Providence, suivis d'un Traité sur les Sacrifices* (Librairie grecque, latine et française, Paris, 1821).

terrible silence falls, and nothing can be heard but the sound of the bones breaking beneath the bar, the yells of the victim. He unties him, places him on a wheel; the shattered members entwine in the spokes; the head hangs down, the hair is on end, and the mouth, gaping like a furnace, no longer emits anything but bloody, intermittent words pleading for death. He has finished; his heart beats, but it is with joy; he applauds himself, he says in his heart: no one uses the wheel better than I. He comes down: he holds out his bloodstained hand, and from a distance, Justice throws a few pieces of gold into it. . . . He sits down at his table, and eats; afterwards goes to bed, and sleeps. And the next day, awakening, thinks of quite other things than what he did the day before. . . ."

The crushing evocation has been attempted with no less evangelical fervour by numberless other *littérateurs*—eager in attendance, most of them, at any execution which might be going, but in print always on the right side of high-mindedness and moral propriety. No one could do a better job of nice feeling in this field than Victor Hugo,[1] revealing with large gestures the private mind of the executioner when there was some talk in France of abolishing the death sentence. "The *bourreau*", we are assured, "was greatly afraid. The day he heard our law-makers talking about humanity, philanthropy, progress, he thought himself lost." A very ingenuous *bourreau* he must have been, if M. Hugo reports him accurately: he should have remembered that the last time these grandiose terms boomed out in relation to capital punishment it was a prelude to the arrival of the guillotine. But M. Hugo is adamant: " . . . he thought himself lost. The wretched creature hid himself, cowered under his guillotine, uneasy in the July sunlight like some night bird in the daytime. . . . But, little by little, there in the shadows about him, he was reassured. He had listened beside the Chamber and had no longer heard his name mentioned. No more of those great

---

[1] See Victor Hugo: *Le dernier jour d'un condamné* (E. Hugues, Paris, 1883).

sonorous words which had so alarmed him. . . . No one any longer gave him a thought, the head-chopper. Seeing this, the man grows calm, he puts his head outside his hole and looks about; he takes a step forward, then two, like a mouse in some fable of La Fontaine, then he risks coming right out from beneath his scaffolding; he jumps up on it, mends it, restores it, polishes it, caresses it, sets it going, shines it, greases the rusty mechanism which disuse has put out of gear; suddenly he swings round, seizes at random by the hair of his head one of the wretches who had hoped to live, pulls him close, strips him, binds him, straps him down. . . ."

But did he ever exist, this demon, this bugaboo? When his son tumbles from the scaffold and breaks his neck, Charles-Henri Sanson displays all the emotion proper to a parent so abruptly bereaved at one stroke of child and apprentice[1]; the tombstone of one of his descendants proclaims him "the benefactor of his whole family who will never cease to pray for him"; [2] burly Heindreicht sobs over the sentimental novels of his day;[3] Roch seeks to minimise the abominable incidentals of death by the guillotine; in the family album, Deibler beams from his new motor-car like any other modest functionary (see Plate XI); during the massacres of St Bartholomew's Day, "one class", says Michelet,[4] "was admirable—that of the executioners. They refused to act, saying that they only killed in conformity with the Law"; his sensibility was such that Le Sénéchal, executioner at Nantes, died within forty-eight hours of guillotining a group of young ladies.[5] Such estimable virtues could never be found in the monsters of de Maistre's imaginings.

And why should he and Hugo consider it so vicious in these wretched mechanics to take satisfaction in a job well done?

[1] See *La Chronique de Paris*, August 29th, 1792.

[2] The Sanson family sepulchre is situated in the Cimetière Montmartre in Paris.

[3] See *Le Petit Moniteur universel*, January 21st, 1870.

[4] See Jules Michelet: *Histoire de France* (17 volumes. Chez Hachette, Chameret, et Chamerot & Lauwereyns, Paris, 1833–67).

[5] See Le Bour'his-Kerbiziet, op. cit.

Why should they be execrated for keeping their tools in sound condition? Hugo himself had witnessed the unpleasing embarrassments which are likely to result from a guillotine improperly set up. Should it stand a fraction off vertical, should the grooves in the uprights not be checked. . . . One recalls the end of that homicidal poet, Lacenaire.[1] To his satisfaction he had been transferred to Paris ("not for anything in the world would I have consented to deal with a provincial headsman"), but when he replaced his accomplice on the platform, the blade dropped thunderously—only not far enough. It was raised again, dropped again: once more it slammed to a halt just above the victim's neck. It was hauled up yet again. With a prodigious effort, Lacenaire twisted his head in time to see the great knife as—at last—it began a successful descent.

Yet it was precisely when more conscientious executioners, bowler-hatted and dark clad, moved softly about in the pre-dawn murk, aligning the *bois de justice* with the aid of spirit-levels, testing the keenness and the rapidity of the knife on bales of straw, that the assembled audience yelled their most wounding witticisms. It outrages one's feelings. What, for instance, could be less deserving of mockery, more worthy of approbation, than the preparations for Campi's execution:[2]

"A gentleman who had kept to one side and whom nobody had noticed until then stepped forward. He seemed to be about forty to forty-five years old. He wore a heavy greatcoat with the collar turned up behind a white silk scarf; his top hat was tilted well back and pushed down onto his ears; his beard was thick and dark-red in colour; he held his two ungloved hands, which toyed with a bunch of little keys, clasped behind his wide back. One could see the cuffs of scarlet wool which projected beneath his sleeves. . . . It was the *bourreau*. . . .

"Coming to the foot of the guillotine, he eyed it from top to bottom, stripped it bare with a glance, possessed it, was

[1] See Pierre Bouchardon: *Crimes d'autrefois* (Perrin & Cie, Paris, 1926).
[2] See Charles Desmaze: *Les Criminels et leurs grâces* (E. Dentu, Paris, 1888).

absorbed in it for a minute or two. Then he touched it, felt it.
caressed it, let his hands wander over it in a satisfied way.
Then, as if to assure himself of its steadiness, he butted it with
his shoulders and his head, casually struck it . . .; he smelt it,
sniffed it, embraced it; he got down on his knees on the footpath as though worshipping it; inspected it from underneath,
almost lying on the ground, using a pretty little dark lantern—
just the sort of lantern for a *bourreau* to carry in his waistcoat
pocket. Then, having leaned the ladder against the uprights,
he climbed quickly to the top as light as snow, tried out the
springs, checked the position of the blade, and, reassured,
came down again, a little tired. Jumping from the middle of
the ladder to the ground, he says in a low voice: 'That'll do'."
One is lost in admiration.

Unhappy *bourreau!* He has, of course, known his hours—
but how rarely, how long ago! During the Terror he was of
impressive consequence—so much so that there were men
pleading to enter the profession. In 1793, the deputy Lequinio
reported from the Charente-Inférieure that "we have set up
a Revolutionary Tribunal here like the one in Paris, and we
ourselves have nominated all the members except the one
who should terminate the process—the *guillotineur*. We wished
to leave to the patriots of Rochefort the glory of freely showing
themselves to be Avengers of the Republic, betrayed by
scoundrels; we revealed the need to the public: 'I!' cried
Citizen Ance with noble enthusiasm, 'I aspire to the honour of
chopping the heads of my country's assassins.' He had hardly
had time to utter these words when others arose with the same
intention and begged to have at least the favour of helping
him; we proclaimed the patriot Ance *guillotineur*, and we
invited him to dine with us, receive his authority in writing
and moisten it with a libation in honour of the Republic."[1]

[1] See *Le Moniteur*, November 13th, 1793. See also Ch. Berriat Saint Prix: *La Justice Révolutionnaire à Paris, Bordeaux, Brest, Lyon, Nantes, Orange, Strasbourg* (Cosse et Marchal, Paris, 1861).

Nor was Ance [1] the only amateur to seek and obtain admission to the guild—but what of it? The Terror did not last for ever, Ance and the other volunteers vanished, and the executioners were again subjected to the familiar obloquy. For that matter, even *during* the Revolution there were ill-disposed louts unable to appreciate a headsman's worth. At the very height of the Terror, on 4 prairial, An II, when executioners were, to quote Sanson, "ready to do all in their power to help maintain the French Republic", the public accuser at Grenoble was forced to come to terms with a couple of convicts in order to have the local sentences carried out. "I have found", he wrote sadly, "that the prejudice against executioners is still deeply rooted in the country." [2]

It remained deeply rooted until the first decade of this century, and vanished then only for a moment. To the benevolent President Fallières must go the credit for briefly establishing a rapport between headsman and public—a quaint Pandarus, in the circumstances, since he was a rigid opponent of capital punishment. It was, moreover, these very principles of his which effected the friendship between the two parties, since, unable to obtain repeal of the law enforcing death sentences, the President, *faute de mieux*, commuted all such sentences to terms of imprisonment. The Parisian public stirred restlessly, and when the atrocious infanticide Soleilland benefited from the presidential clemency, cries of "*Vive la guillotine! Vive Deibler!*" sounded along the boulevards. Suddenly he, Deibler, the *bourreau, coupe-tête*, was a popular hero; songs were written in his praise, he was saluted in broadsheets; the satiric periodicals of the day, for whom he had always been a favourite target, left him alone and went to work on the President. He, whose name had become a synonym for his office, found himself regarded as the defender of

----

[1] His name is also given as Hanss and as Hentz. There is some reason to think that he was of German origin and that his name was in fact Hentz.

[2] See Lenotre, op. cit.

terrified society—for, oddly enough, the public is often less panic-stricken by a full-scale war than by a private gentleman with homicidal tastes, even though the latter at his best can only, like Dr Petiot, say, chalk up a beggarly sixty-three to his score.

The rumpus over Soleilland had its effect; exercise of the presidential prerogative became less whole-hearted; murderers were once more likelier to end on the guillotine rather than in the "dry guillotine"—the barracks of Guiana; and, incomprehensibly, the truce between executioner and public was at an end. No sooner was he engaged in carrying out the sentences which the people obdurately demanded than he was again consigned to that category of untouchableness with which his kind were so well acquainted.

And how absolute, that condition! Maton de la Varenne, writing in 1790, evokes the memory of Jacques Ganier, executioner at Rennes until thirty years before. The delicate fellow never went to work without first taking communion, it seems; he was prodigal in kindnesses to the poor; he was a courteous but firm referee at the local magistrates' games of *boule*: small wonder that his death was regarded as "a public calamity", that the population wept in the streets and that, during years to follow, "his tomb was visited like that of a saint".[1]

But not many *bourreaux* have been able to bask in such esteem, even though, as Maton de la Varenne reminds us, "their knowledge of surgery . . . often effected cures for which all hope had been abandoned". Jacques Ganier remains a Rennais oddity, his popularity in astonishing contrast with the revulsion encountered by his colleagues. France has long manifested a distaste for these functionaries, unlike Germany (always according to La Varenne) where "the office is considered one of the most important", or England, where the executioners "are regarded as citizens of note" and where

---

[1] See Maton de la Varenne: *Mémoire pour les exécuteurs des jugemens criminels de toutes les villes du royaume, où l'on prouve la légitimité de leur état* (Paris, 1790).

they "encounter no barrier to other professions and are received with pleasure by one and all".

In France, on the other hand, "they exist only to suffer humiliation, shame and opprobrium". It is incontestable. No sooner had Grohot, executioner at Chambéry, drunk and paid for his apéritif in a local café than the proprietor ostentatiously smashed the tainted glass on the floor.[1] In pre-Revolutionary days when the headsman was entitled to a proportion of all foodstuffs reaching the local market, he was required to serve himself by means of a long metal spoon: his dishonoured hands would infect the produce were he to touch it.[2] His house must be situated at some distance from his neighbours.[3] No society was available to him but that of his own assistants or his fellow-headsmen. Innumerable local decrees and finally the order of the King in Council [4] could not protect him from the public's use of the pejorative term "bourreau". And was it as a concession to him or to other potential conscripts that in 1799 he was exempted from all military service? [5]

Unhappy bourreau! He has argued that he should be looked on as no more than what his official title proclaims him to be— the executioner of sentences imposed by others. He could claim with much less speciousness than Fouquier-Tinville: "Je suis la hache! On ne punit pas la hache!" The jury which finds an accused man guilty and piously abstains from recommending mercy is commended for its lofty sense of duty; the judge who pronounces sentence of death is a welcome dinner guest; the ill-paid official who practices what they preach is execrated by the whole of the society which insists on his existence. Only the Roman Catholic Church displays a proper sense of proportion in declaring the judge who has delivered a capital sentence to be as "irregular" as the headsman.

[1] See Le Petit Moniteur universel, January 21st, 1870.
[2] See Lenotre, op. cit., and others.
[3] See Le Bour'his-Kerbiziet, op. cit., and others.
[4] Arrêté du 12 janvier, 1787.
[5] Arrêté du Directoire exécutif du 13 floréal, an VII (May 2nd, 1799).

Under the monarchy it was demanded of the aspiring
executioner that he should furnish, in addition to adequate
proof of his sound morals, a certificate that he was also a
member of the Roman Catholic Church; under the Republic,
this latter requirement has been waived. The fact that Rome
lumps him in with the upper echelons of his country's magistracy can therefore be only a minor consolation.

For, conditioned from generation to generation to see himself as an ignoble and revolting personage, he has acquired a
ponderous sense of guilt. Like well-loved Ganier, Heindreicht
was a devoted communicant; but while the rest of the congregation came forward, as required, with bare hands, he was
solicitous to put on his gloves. And Louis Deibler was only
one member of his profession who suffered from hæmophobia
—a pathological aversion to blood. It was he who, after the
execution of Carrara, collapsed suddenly at the foot of the
guillotine screaming that he was covered with the stuff.
Ridiculous, of course: a practical shield is provided to guard
against just such unpleasantnesses.

The unvarying hostility of a sanctimonious populace tempts
one to represent the executioners as being all as virtuous as
M. Ganier. It would not be accurate, naturally, and they
would be less human—less like ourselves—if it were so. They
had their faults, it must be admitted. Ance, for example, had
an unseemly relish for his job,[1] and there was that Versailles
bourreau of whom the local police reported [2] in 1821 that he
was guilty of "the most infamous conduct, an inveterate
drunkard, insolent, loaded with debts . . . a man dwelling
in filth, who prides himself on his station in life; at all executions he affects a gaiety which arouses the public's indignation.
. . ." A bad lot, there is no denying; and his depravity went
still further, for, as the same report reveals, "since it is a day of

---

[1] See Biré, op. cit.
[2] See Albert Terrade: *La guillotine et ses divers emplacements à Versailles*
(C. Bernard, Versailles, 1903).

d his assistants whenever there is an
to the extent of cooking a calf's head
t publicly transported to the local café
completes a sorry story. There is no
shows a want of tact.

Not all the headsmen, happily, were as boisterous as M. de Versailles, but few of them (one speaks of the past) were wholly without blemish. There was among them a regrettable tendency to alcoholism, causing the dismissal of quite a number and their behaviour was sometimes lacking in refinement. Indicative of this occasional discourtesy is a message from the *Directoire* on September 21st, 1796, which refers to the fact that "there have been several complaints in respect of the atrociously insolent manner displayed by these officers of the law in carrying out their executions". There had indeed. Only two years before, the Citizen Captain Hausson had been moved to protest that when he made a perfectly reasonable suggestion to the Citizen Desmorets, a well-known executioner, the latter had "insolently replied that he had not got to take orders from me and that the matter was his own business. . . ."[1]

As a rule, the keepers of the guillotine sought to perform their duties with as little unpleasantness for all concerned as was consistent with their releasing the blade, but an occasional brutality must be added to the list of their shortcomings. The police informer, Latour-Lamontagne, was obliged to report[2] on 7 ventôse, An II, that audiences had been shocked by the ferocity with which the executioner sometimes acted. He had "grabbed hold of several criminals with a violence which revolted many spectators"—but the fellow was overworked at the time, and perhaps it was carelessness rather than savagery which led to this display.

And, similarly, much is made of the treatment accorded Robespierre by the headsman, without anyone pausing to

[1] See Fleischmann, op. cit.   [2] Ibid.

consider whether the latter might not have been motivat҃
something other than mere sadism. The Incorruptible had ҃
his jaw smashed at the Hôtel de Ville by an exuberant gen-
darme; quite gratuitously (as it would seem) Sanson wrenched
off the bandage supporting it; Robespierre's scream was audible
far away.[1] But may not the executioner have been a Dan-
tonist? With the *bourreau* it is too easy to detect brutality in
actions which, with other men, would be taken as no more
than indications of rigid principle.

When all is said and done, one must agree with Mme
Roland: the headsman does his job and is paid for it. The King
and the Queen and the King's mistress; Robespierre and
Danton; aristocrats and commoners; saints and criminals:
Sanson decapitated them all with (in the main) splendid impar-
tiality, just as Desfourneaux in our own day was to function
untroubled before the Occupation, during it and after—perhaps the only official who was instinctively recognised to be
beyond such issues as resistance or collaboration.

[1] See Jules Mazé: *Sous la Terreur* (Hachette, Paris, 1947).

Jacques Delarue

An execution in 1908. At left the cart in which the body will
be transported to the autopsy

PLATE IX

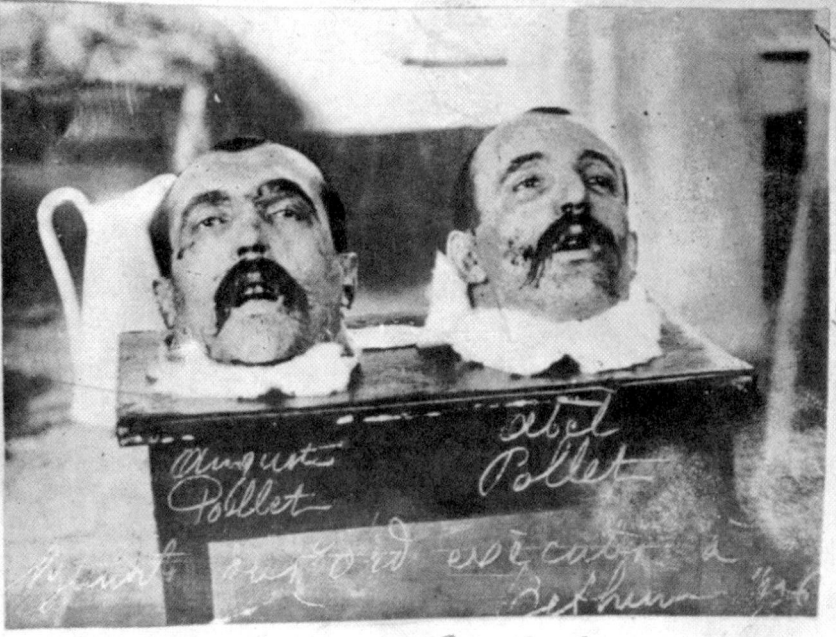

Photo : Jacques Delarue

The heads of Auguste and Abel Pollet, *les chauffeurs de la Drôme*,
executed January 11th, 1909

PLATE X

CHAPTER ELEVEN

IN 1795 some of the one hundred and sixty executioners then at work in France petitioned the *Convention nationale* on behalf of themselves and their colleagues for an increase in salary.[1] Among the signatories were MM. Desmorets, Desfourneaux, Berger, Etienne and Ganier;[2] among the non-signatories whose interests the others were representing was Antoine Roch, headsman at Briey.

In 1843, Nicolas Roch, grandson of Antoine, replaced François Desmorets as executioner at Lons-le-Saulnier.

In 1853, he was promoted to executioner at Amiens in succession to Henri Ganier.

In 1872, by then occupying the post of executioner at Paris itself, his five assistants included MM. Berger, Ganier and Desfourneaux.

In 1952, the grandson of this last died in Paris, efficiently carrying out the duties of executioner to the end.

Until 1952, in other words, there was never a moment when one or more of the names appearing on that petition to the *Convention* was not to be found listed in connection with the business of official decapitation, and this example of the

---

[1] Quoted by Lenotre, op. cit.

[2] The name appears on the document as Garnié, but certainly refers to a descendant of that Jacques Ganier mentioned by Maton de la Varenne. The spelling of the executioners' names is often very haphazard. This particular family appears as Ganier, Gasnier, Garnier, Garnié and Ganié. Similarly, Heindreicht—as he himself signed all the official papers which I have seen—is sometimes alluded to as Heindenreich, sometimes as Hendricht, and so on. I have adopted a uniform spelling throughout.

same names recurring among the *bourreaux* could be multiplied almost endlessly. The post of Questioner, Executioner of the High Works, Peoples' Avenger, Executioner of the Criminal Sentences—the *bourreau* has enjoyed a great range of grandiose titles at different periods—has always been preserved, in fact if not in law, for the same families. Vast dynasties have effortlessly taken over the office from generation to generation like Whig nobles sharing out Cabinet appointments. On occasion, in fact, the process has been on a still higher level than the mere hereditary acquisition of office and has come more to resemble the inheritance of kingship. Not even the Russells, as far as one knows, were selected as future Prime Ministers while still in their cradles or charged before they had entered their teens with the post of Foreign Secretary; such precocious doings have always been restricted to royalty and, as it happens, to headsmen. In Paris in 1766, Charles-Jean-Baptiste Sanson came into the title at the age of seven, François Prud'homme being named regent until the boy should reach his majority; at Epernay, Simon Jean was scarcely older when he succeeded to his father, and Simon Desmorets, the young *bourreau's* uncle, left his own scaffold at Chalons-en-Champagne to guide the lad's early steps.[1]

It is impossible to say with any precision how far back this dynastic tradition extends. In 1793, Nicolas-Richard Jouënne was confessing to an understandable pride in the fact that his forebears had, like himself, been executioners at Caudebec-en-Caux for two centuries; the first Sanson known to have occupied the post was functioning in the sixteen-hundreds; the Desfourneaux are said to have been chopping and mutilating their kind since the fourteenth century. All that one can attest is that for at least two hundred years—and in certain cases for much longer—the same families carried out the same lugubrious task: Desmorets, Ferey, Etienne, Ganier, Roch, Sanson, Jouënne, Rasseneux, Deibler, Heindreicht, Canné: there are

[1]   See Lenotre, op. cit.

few of these who could not beat the bulk of Debrett's nominees when it came to establishing for how long their ancestors had disposed of an hereditary office.

If only the whimsical German method of choosing executioners [1] had been employed, these dynasties might never have emerged. With the Germans, it was the most recently married man in the vicinity, the most recently arrived or the youngest magistrate of the district who was required to apply the penalties demanded by the law. It may have made for a hesitancy in entering into matrimony; it may have discouraged migration from town to town; it may have made recruitment for the magistracy more difficult; but it tended to prevent the institution of family cartels in the field of capital punishment.[2]

Since no such lucky dip existed in France, the Jouënnes, the Sansons, the Etiennes and the rest came into being; but the question remains as to how the founders of the clans first came to take up their profession. Can it have been out of political principle, as with the amateur executioners of the Revolution, and, if so, what more creditable? Was it a matter of avocation —that spontaneous enthusiasm which is said to have caused the infant Deibler to spend so much time at the Nuremberg Museum of Tortures in his native Bavaria? Were they attracted by the perquisites of the office, which, as will be seen, were often considerable? Perhaps the likeliest explanation is that, since feudal lords had the right to order and have carried out any sentence they thought appropriate, some husky-looking serf was haphazardly selected to take over the necessary torturing or slaughtering and that his descendants were thereby condemned to the same career.

Once having entered the guild, what escape could there be? Who would wish to employ the *bourreau's* son or the *bourreau's* brother? The family whose chief had once served society as

[1] See Maton de la Varenne, op. cit.
[2] Not invariably, however. The Deiblers, for example, were a family which spawned numerous headsmen in Germany before shifting to France.

executioner was henceforth damned, committed for generations after to the same function. There have been spasmodic
efforts by various members of the great clans to escape from
their destiny, but how rarely they have succeeded. Louis-
Henri-Gabriel Sanson, son, grandson, great-grandson, great-
great-grandson, nephew, cousin and uncle of executioners,
heroically triumphed over the weight of his alliances and
extricated himself from the profession. It would be fascinating
—horribly so, no doubt—to know what his evasion cost him,
what changes of name, what changes of address, how many lost
positions and lost friends; and to no end except that he
and his wife and children were "isolated from all society by
the fact of the father's profession . . . and although of
irreproachable conduct are in a state of penury".[1]

More typical is the case of Anatole Deibler, who likewise
determined that his family's predestined profession should
cease with him. Exempt from the need to undergo military
training, he insisted, nagged, pleaded until he had obtained
the privilege—as it was for him—of peeling potatoes for his
country. Only there was his name: to be called Deibler was as
though one were to be called M. Coupe-Tête. It was incon-
ceivable that a Deibler was not by nature a drinker of blood:
he was an object of derision, distrust, fear. He quitted the
regiment and found employment in a department store under
an assumed name. Hopeless subterfuge! In no time at all, every
shop-walker, every clerk and bookkeeper knew him for what
he was—a Deibler, an innate, ordained, congenital killer. He
surrendered. He rejoined his father as assistant in the family
trade. Before his death he had chopped more heads than he
himself could remember.

It would seem as though nothing but death can liberate the
born executioners from meeting their obligations, and yet
none of them has committed suicide. And, as strangely, none

[1] Report from the Prefect of the Seine-et-Marne, quoted by Lenotre,
op. cit.

has preferred crime to the performance of legal homicide. None of the great clans, at any rate. Two Lyonnais executioners found guilty of murder were decapitated with their own tools in 1794,[1] but their names, Ripet and Bernard, do not belong to the register of the illustrious executing families. And one can hardly count Hespel the Jackal, headsman in the Guiana penal settlement, who also ended under the knife of the guillotine.[2] The true executioners, conscious of a responsibility to the immortal names they bear, have never indulged in any serious antisocial activity but have quietly fulfilled their duties from father to son.

And not only from father to son. As with all aristocratic families, provision is made for the cadet branches. At twenty, attending his first execution, Nicolas Roch was assisting his Uncle Pierre as well as his father, François; at one period in the nineteenth century, all seven of the Sanson brothers were actively and simultaneously engaged in the profession. Among executioners, uncles and nephews, cousins and second cousins enjoy shared memories.

Not to mention mothers, wives, aunts and sisters; for the female line is as inextricably involved in this fatal continuity as the male. For a young woman to marry a headsman is almost automatically to condemn her sisters and nieces and cousins to remain spinsters or to accept helpmates following the same profession. Hence the parents of ladies who show signs of a *tendresse* towards a *bourreau* can be relied on to oppose the union with even more fervour than parents usually manifest when daughters select their mates. There are innumerable examples of eligible executioners frustrated in their natural desires by the intended parents-in-law, and never have these

[1] See Lenotre, op. cit.

[2] See L. Le Boucher: *Ce qu'il faut connaître du bagne* (Boivin & Cie, Paris, 1930). As always in the penal settlements, the executioner was chosen from among the convicts. Hespel le Chacal was for long a commendable functionary and, when finally condemned to death for the murder of a fellow convict, asked for and obtained a last recognition of his services. He was permitted to set up the guillotine for his own execution.

latter been persuaded to change their minds, even by so convincing a letter [1] as that sent by the present headsman, M. André Obrecht, to the father of his first love :

"You are opposed to capital punishment and you make this clear by refusing your daughter's hand to a *bourreau*; it is a point of view. But if you were to come home one night and find your wife murdered, your daughter strangled and the murderer still in the house and about to escape—what would you do? You have a revolver in your pocket: will you fire or not?

"If you accept this act of private justice, how can you not accept what I do on behalf of legal justice? I punish criminals, I frighten off those tempted to become criminals, but I have the support of a court and I only punish murderers."

M. Obrecht's unassailable argument had no effect. He was compelled to look elsewhere for a bride, and that he found one having no connections with the trade makes him a rarity among those of his calling. Ordinarily who would want to marry the executioner if not some other executioner's sister or daughter? After whom could the executioner's ardent sister or daughter presume to yearn if not one of her male relation's colleagues or assistants? The dismal commingling of these tribes parodies a more than royal exclusiveness. The founder of the Sanson line took to wife the daughter of his opposite number at Caudebec-en-Caux; Nicolas Roch's eldest daughter married her father's aide; the amateur executioner of Revolutionary days, Jacques Collet de Charmoy, arranged a wedding between his sister and one of the Sansons; Ernould Outredebanque, assistant headsman at Arras, whose family had had a good hundred years in the trade, linked his lot with that of the daughter of the Cambrai headsman, Vermeil—a name no less glorious in the same field.

If one only knew a little more about these gruesome ladies, if only one had some record of the conversations when their husbands returned home after a morning's work! Females

[1] Quoted by Danjou, op. cit.

have always shown themselves worthy companions to the more rugged male in the matter of bloodletting, as certain Revolutionary police reports [1] sufficiently demonstrate. "It is astonishing", according to one such document, "to what an extent the women have become ferocious", and, according to another, "the women have become so bloodily inclined that they rejoice in nothing but blood".

We knew too little of the women who, not content to be spectators merely, claimed and obtained the right to participate in the removal of heads. When one thinks of Mme Grosseholtz, who was designated assistant to her husband,[2] of the "bourelle" who, in 1615, took over the somewhat happy-go-lucky slaughter of a young girl when the male executioner's nerve failed him [3]—how one longs for some really detailed information! And coming to the epoch of the guillotine, what a satisfaction it would be to learn something more of Marie Ferey, daughter of a headsman, sister of a headsman, widow of a headsman, who, when her husband, Jacques-Joseph Ganier, passed away, herself stoutly maintained the family business— and to the contentment of all impartial observers.[4]

Most of all, however, one would wish to obtain some intimate portrait of the dim little ladies who, although non-practitioners themselves, linked their lives with those of the bourreaux. As it is, we know almost nothing of any but Mme Roch, and little enough of her—declining to be put upon when her late husband's successor tried to seize that collection of blades, and gently boasting that "they may find someone to do work as good as Nicolas, but never anyone to do better".[5]

Just how much is owed to the female branch can be seen in the case of M. André Obrecht. He was chosen from more than four hundred applicants when the post fell vacant in 1951,

[1] Quoted by Fleischmann, op. cit.
[2] See Lenotre, op. cit.
[3] See Taschereau: *Revue Rétrospective*, t. II, 1834.
[4] See Le Bour'his-Kerbiziet, op. cit.
[5] See Grison, op. cit.

and it is a permissible guess that the responsible authorities were at least as much influenced by his distinguished lineage as by the fact that he had, in the capacity of assistant executioner, familiarised himself with the necessary procedure. He is tortuously related to his predecessor, Henri Desfourneaux, last of that immortal name, and to his predecessor's predecessor, Anatole Deibler; through the Desfourneaux he is connected with the Sansons, through the Deiblers with the Rasseneux; he is linked with the Rogis, of proven competence as assistant executioners.

All this distinction is due to his mother, Juliette Rogis. But for her . . . His father, Jean-Baptiste, was an intimate of executioners, it is true—Monsieur de Paris was a witness at his wedding, and he had filled the same rôle a few years earlier at the wedding of Monsieur de Paris—but he was not of the caste. He was, in fact, a tailor, and only through his wife has he succeeded in establishing his name on the great records of judicial homicide: Obrecht may yet become as illustrious a patronymic as Deibler, as Etienne, as Ferey, as Sanson.

It is encouraging to look over the different civil documents concerned with these families, the certificates of birth, marriage, death. In them the survival of the dynastic tradition becomes more and more manifest. To discover that the death of Heindreicht in 1872 was announced to the local *mairie* by a Berger and a Desfourneaux; to find that it is the same Léon Berger who makes the same dismal constatation seven years later in respect of Nicolas Roch; to see that a Deibler and his assistant were witnesses to the joyous news that Anatole Deibler, most renowned of his line, had been born; to observe that forty-seven years later it is Anatole who in turn signs the birth certificate of his destined successor, Henri Desfourneaux; to meet once more with the fine old name of Ganier among those present at the wedding of M. André Obrecht—amidst the tottering of aristocracies all this provides an element of stability and continuity which one might have thought was gone from the world.

CHAPTER TWELVE

Nof the good executing families has achieved so certain
a place in history as the Sansons. It is not just abject
respect for a name distinguished in civil service activities since
the seventeenth century which is involved, and a snob
would certainly give preference to the Desfourneaux, who
are of still greater antiquity. Nor is it simply because one of
the Sansons was chosen to decapitate Louis XVI that one
is impressed, although there is, of course, a natural appeal in
this intimate connection between two such socially exclusive
families as the Sansons and the Capets. Their charm, in fact, is
unaccountable, but it is no less real for that, and any study of
the guillotine and its guardians must accord them a suitable
prominence.

The trouble is that practically nothing is known about them.
Most of those who met them at close quarters had no time to
record their impressions; and the volume of memoirs [1]
ostensibly by Charles-Henri Sanson is in reality by many
hands, Balzac's among them, but Sanson's not at all. Outside
one or two official documents and those letters written after
the King's execution, no correspondence has been preserved.
All of them performed in public, yet no one in their enormous
audiences thought to note down the details of their com-
portment and appearance. The last of the practising members

---

[1] *Mémoires pour servir à l'histoire de la Révolution française, par Sanson,
exécuteur des arrêts criminels pendant la Révolution* (Librairie centrale, Paris,
1829).

of the family died as recently as 1889, and it might as well have been a thousand years ago.

The very birthplace of the first Sanson—Charles Sanson, known as Longval—is uncertain: the credit has been given to places as far apart as Northern Italy and Picardy. According to one writer,[1] the great man was born at Abbeville, but no authority is given for the assertion. Then, he is said to have been a lieutenant in the army of La Boissière, governor of Dieppe (which implies a degree of gentility not always found in the origins of eminent families), but we are not told in what Army Lists his name occurs.[2] Above all, no conclusive answer has ever been provided to the question of how an officer and a gentleman (if he was that) happened to transfer to the executing business.

His marriage to Marguerite Jouënne, daughter of the executioner at Caudebec-en-Caux and by whom he had one son, is usually considered a sufficient explanation. But why did he marry her? Was his ardour so feverish that he was ready to make a marriage which would (as he must have known in advance) thereafter debar him from the exercise of any *métier* but that of his father-in-law? Or was it less deliciously impulsive? Might dashing Lieutenant Sanson have dealt with the headsman's daughter . . . lightly? It is a chilling thought, but was the headsman perhaps obliged to remind young Sanson that even headsmen's daughters have a reputation to lose?

But perhaps, too, for some unknown reason (gambling debts? It seems suitably doggish and military) he had already changed professions before his marriage. In that case he would have been doomed to look for a wife in executing circles. There is no way of finding out which caused the other—whether the marriage begot the axe, or the axe the marriage. The tender problem is only the first of many obscurities in the story.

---

[1] See du Bois, op. cit.   [2] Ibid.

The first definite date available is September 23rd, 1688, when Charles Sanson was granted a royal commission to take over the Paris slaughterings. It is to his credit that so important a post should have been bestowed on him, having no direct family connections with the mystery, rather than on one of his wife's relations with all their awesome hereditary associations. He must have learned fast.

On his death in 1707, his place was filled by his son, also Charles. The old gentleman had married twice, the second time with a Jeanne-Renée Dubut, and young Charles took the somewhat unusual course of marrying his stepmother's sister, Marthe. There is no record of the Dubuts as executioners in their own right, but the women of the family clearly had a natural feeling for the business. That the two sisters should each choose to marry an executioner is already proof of a special matrimonial taste; but that Marthe, on Charles junior's death in 1726, should remarry with Jean Barré, another headsman, makes the whole thing epic. One would like to know more about such high-spirited girls.

At precise three-year intervals, three children were born to Charles and Marthe. A daughter, Anne-Renée, doubtless feeling that the situation was getting out of hand, succeeded in breaking away from tradition and married a musician, Christian Zelle, with whom she settled decorously at Soissons. It is impossible not to sympathise with the effort; but the Sanson blood, mingled so grandly with the blood of Jouënnes and Dubuts, could not be denied. Music never stood a chance against head-chopping, and, until the Revolution, all Christian's descendants worked unspectacularly but efficiently in their native town with sword and wheel and axe.

The two boys, Anne-Renée's brothers, never even attempted to do other than submissively follow their father's trade. The youngest, Nicolas-Charles-Gabriel, took over the branch at Reims, where, in due course, he was succeeded by *his* son, Jean-Louis; the eldest, as was only right, got Paris. It was this last, Charles-Jean-Baptiste, who was nominated to the office when aged seven (the authorities refusing to let the little chap practise, however, until he was twenty-one),[1] but it is the lady who became his wife about whom one would really like some information. She was, we are told, the daughter of his guardian, but that is no help at all. Who was she, this Madeleine Tronson? It is intolerable not to know. For it was from her loins that there came the seven prodigious sons who were one and all to become executioners, three of whom were themselves to beget executioners (one of them by the sister of the amateur headsman of the Revolution, Collet de Charmoy), and the eldest of whom was to be the first man to use the guillotine and the only man to use it on a king.[2]

At Tours, at Reims, at Montpellier, in Paris; at Dijon, at Provins, at Angers—in each town, a Sanson. What if one of them was ultimately dismissed for drunkenness? What if another servilely referred to his brother's royal victim as "the Tyrant"? Nothing can mar the grandeur of this fabulous fraternity. Tours, Reims, Montpellier. . . .

Yet, once again, how little—how tragically little is known of them. And if only one could be sure that the few available scraps of information were authentic. Those family dinners, for example, when all the brothers would assemble at the Sanson house in the rue Neuve-Saint-Jean under the twinkling direction of Grandmother Marthe: they have been beautifully described, one would love to believe in them. But is it possible? However united in spirit, the brothers were geographically scattered; a trip to Paris from Montpellier, say, involved some days' journeying; executions would never have been left by such craftsmen to mere assistants: can it have ever happened that during the time necessary for such a reunion to take place,

[1] See Lenotre, op. cit.
[2] It has been suggested that it was not in fact this Sanson, Charles-Henri, who executed the King, but his son, Henry. For a variety of reasons, it seems likelier that both were concerned with the matter, Henry probably acting as his father's assistant.

all seven brothers were simultaneously without any work on hand in their various parishes?

It may be true that their aides distinguished the members of this gargantuan group from each other by calling them after the towns in which they operated—M. de Tours, M. de Reims, M. de Montpellier and so on. And it may be true that the quasi-official title of M. de Paris, still used of the one executioner now available for all France and whose head-quarters, of course, are in the capital, derives from this pretty practice. One would have thought that M. Charles, M. Louis, M. Cyr would have done just as well, but headsmen's assistants may have a whimsicality of their own.

It would be gratifying to know something about each of the Sanson brothers, and one would be ready to make do with a really comprehensive account of just the eldest—Charles-Henri, executioner of the King. It is incredible, but a bare century and a half after his memorable performance it is as though he never existed. We are given a glimpse of him at the Théâtre du Vaudeville, and the writer [1] who provides it was astonished that an executioner should be able to laugh at the antics on the stage; like any other government official, he complains repeatedly that he is inadequately paid, but his memoranda on the subject stick to the material facts and reveal nothing of his thoughts or sentiments: the shadowy creature eludes one always.

M. Begin,[2] always splendidly authoritative, describes him on his arrival at Great-Uncle Antoine Louis' house for that historic conference about the guillotine: "Sanson was a fine figure of a man, his face calm and devoid of any hardness. His clothes, without being unduly studied, were nonetheless of some elegance. He was polite in his behaviour, and his manner of speaking was as simple as it was correct. He was clearly a

---

[1] See L. S. Mercier: *Le Nouveau Paris* (Fuchs, C. Pougens and C.-F. Cramer, Paris, 1798).
[2] Begin MS.

well-brought-up man": but M. Begin cannot himself have
laid eyes on this paragon, and Uncle Antoine is not likely to
have spoken so warmly of anyone.

A foreign visitor [1] who was imprisoned in Paris during the
Terror has left a yet more vivid portrait. Coming into the
gaoler's room on one occasion, she found him "sitting at a
table with a very handsome, smart young man, drinking wine.
The gaoler told me to sit down and drink a glass too. I did not
dare to refuse. The young man said, 'Well I must be off' and
looked at his watch. The gaoler replied, No; your work will
not begin till twelve o'clock.' I looked at the young man, and
the gaoler said to me, 'You must make friends with this citizen;
it is young Samson [sic] the executioner, and perhaps it may fall
to his lot to behead you.' I felt quite sick, especially when he
took hold of my throat saying, it will soon be off your neck,
it is so long and small. If I am to despatch you, it will be
nothing but a squeeze'." But Charles-Henri at that epoch was
no longer "a very handsome young man" but a mature
executioner of between fifty and sixty years of age. It may, of
course, have been his son whom Miss Elliott encountered—
unless the whole incident was invented or she was the victim
of the turnkey's humour.

No, the portraits are unconvincing and only by inference
can one know anything about Charles-Henri Sanson. He seems
to have had an orderly mind: that much can be deduced from
his letter setting out the circumstances of the King's execution;
but it was presumably *amour-propre* which impelled him to
have the word "*bourreau*" declared defamatory; and his court
action against the journalist Gorsas was obviously dictated by
self-interest, pure and simple.

Why not? In December of 1789, the *Assemblée Constituante*
was exercised with the question of the electoral laws and the

[1] See Grace Dalrymple Elliott: *During the Reign of Terror. Journal of my
life during the French Revolution* (T. Fisher Unwin, London, 1910). Miss
Elliott's rather personal system of punctuation has been left unaltered.

eligibility or ineligibility of different members of the public. Demonstrating a splendid freedom from prejudice (or did they already foresee how dependent they were to become on the fellow for the implementation of their reforms?) the deputies decided that the executioner should be treated like any other honourable citizen. Sagacious deputies! One can imagine their hurt astonishment when, almost simultaneously, it was discovered that in a house belonging to the *bourreau*, aristocrats were engaged in printing subversive pamphlets.

What a scandal it must have been! Gorsas sprang vindictively on the news; [1] the rest of the journalists followed him; feverishly maintaining his lead, Gorsas announced that all the headsmen of France, abjectly attached to their feudal past, were linked in a vast conspiracy to restore the *ancien régime*.

But at his interrogation, Sanson was able to clear the whole affair up. He had, it appeared, out of sheer benevolence, made part of his house available to some poor workmen of the district; he had no knowledge of what had been going on and "I do not think I am in any way compromised". Neither did his judges. He was acquitted of all complicity. He instituted proceedings against Gorsas for libel and the latter was ordered to retract his allegations.

"Victim of a misconception which has existed since time began," wrote Gorsas[2] in one of the least conciliatory apologies on record, "I retract, O Charles-Henri Sanson, *bourreau* of Paris, my fellow-citizen!!!! . . . Come, Charles-Henri Sanson, come, take your seat in one of our assemblies. YOU ARE ELIGIBLE! Perhaps you want a vote? I will give you mine: you shall be an elector! you shall be elected! Who knows? Perhaps you will become a member of the *Assemblée nationale*! You will become its president. . . ."

All such spilling of bile could not alter the fact that Sanson had triumphed. The trouble into which his charity had already

[1] See *Le Courrier de Paris*, t. VII, No. XIX, Mercredi, 30 Décembre, 1789.
[2] See *Le Courrier de Paris*, t. IX, No. VIII, Jeudi, 11 Fevrier, 1790.

landed him did not deter him from asking that the damages obtained from cross-grained Gorsas should be distributed to the poor people of his quarter: a further disdainful gesture against the journalist. And through all this litigation, in the face of all the questioning, despite the necessity of bespeaking himself, somehow Sanson managed to conceal his personality still. Can it be that there was no personality to reveal other than that of a dim old philanthropist?

Towards the end of the century, a troublesome nephritis obliged Charles-Henri Sanson to retire from the service. He was succeeded by his son, Henry, and it is perhaps unnecessary to mention that significant data concerning him is scarcely more abundant than in regard to his father. A number of people had the privilege of visiting 31 *bis* rue des Marais where Henry, *his* son, Clément-Henri, and the assistant executioners all lived together in dolorous promiscuity; but each of these visitors managed to bungle his opportunity most lamentably.

Among them was Alexandre Dumas *père*,[1] who was professionally interested to obtain a first-hand account of the execution of Louis XVI. For some reason he decided that he must offer some alternative explanation for his call and, recollecting that the *bourreau* ran a spare-time business of selling healing unguents,[2] he presented himself in the guise of a kindly nonentity with a relative who suffered from rheumatism. Henry produced the ointment, informed his client that the price was dependent on the buyer's means, and asked, "Is that all you want?"

"No", replied M. Dumas with bluff candour. "There is something else, only I hardly like to ask you. But," he added quickly, "I am not just anybody."

[1] See Alexandre Dumas (the elder): *Causeries, 2ième série* (Michel Lévy frères, Paris, 1860).

[2] This was a traditional side-line among the *bourreaux*. Their ointments were reputedly made of the blood and fat of their victims and possessed of amazing curative properties (see Le Bour'his-Kerbiziet, op. cit.).

Photo : Jacques Delarue

Louis Deibler, chief executioner, with his wife

PLATE XI

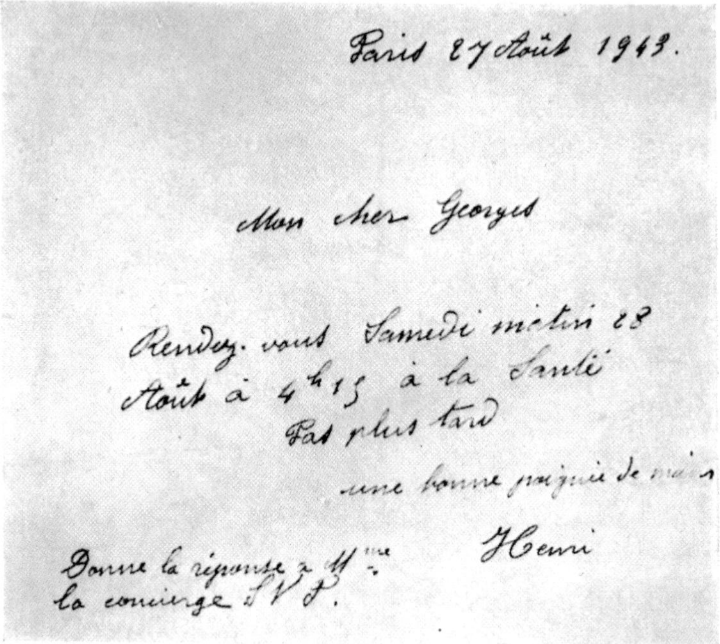

A note from Henri Desfourneaux, chief executioner,
requesting his assistant's presence at an execution to
take place at the Santé prison

PLATE XII

"Tell me your name or not, as you wish", said the *bourreau* indifferently.

M. Dumas hesitated. "I am the author", he said coyly, "of *Henri III, Christine* and *Antony*."

Dramatic moment! The *bourreau's* reaction was exactly right. "Ah, M. Dumas! What a pity that my son is out! He's a great theatre-goer."

Et voilà tout. Henry confirmed the details of the King's death already set down by his father; he conducted M. Dumas through the family museum—"a veritable arsenal of axes, *doloires*, head-choppers of all sorts"—where the great man was permitted to handle the sword used at the execution of Lally; he lamented again the absence of his stage-struck son; and the visit was ended.

The journalist, James Rousseau,[1] likewise dropped in at the rue des Marais establishment and his account of the occasion is no less disappointing. Henry was a courteous old gentleman, we are informed (M. Dumas had wonderingly commented on the executioner's "gentle, melancholy and venerable countenance"); he "did not seek to conceal the horror of the position in which fate had placed him"; he had so lively a sense of his own spiritual isolation that he declined to dip his fingers in the other's snuff-box; he provided—if M. Rousseau quotes him correctly—some vastly inexact tales of bygone executions. . . . It might as well have been a visit to an eccentric rural dean.

Fortunately there is a little more known about his son, Clément-Henri. Only a little—but what an engaging picture it is which emerges! Blithe Clément! He is like one of the *bourreaux* in Giraudoux's *Intermezzo*, waggish, jovially unashamed of his profession, ready to defend it with shrewdness and good humour. And what a man of the world, what a dog! If only attendance at M. Dumas' first nights were his utmost dissipation; but he was an incorrigible spendthrift, an enthusiastic

[1] His account is quoted *in extenso* by Lenotre, op. cit.

connoisseur of vintages, happily admitted that he was a slave to women. An engaging picture; but highly unsatisfactory from his masters' point of view. Steadiness and sobriety are essential in the good headsman. After a mere seven years in office, Clément Sanson was dismissed.

A Sanson dismissed, and the last of the family at that—for Clément had no son—it is a wretched ending for so great a family. And there is no excuse. Clément had every advantage which a headsman could desire—generations of honest craftsmen behind him, a wife (the daughter of that fine executioner, Charles-Constant Desmorets) who shared his professional interests, a constant inspiration from his toddler days in that private museum of blades and cleavers.

M. Dumas attributes his ruin to the fact that whenever an execution was ordered Clément could not be found; Canler himself, chief of the *Sûreté*, was forever sleuthing through the *mauvais lieux* of Paris in search of the gamesome *bourreau*. After a few such annoyances, says M. Dumas, Clément was retired.

Better for Clément had it been so; the facts are even more discreditable. He had gone through his inheritance (a considerable one) like a Regency buck. His sportive nature demanded distraction as insistently as ever. The theatre—Dumas' latest—his ladies, his wine—they all cost money. Out of sheer good nature (one may surmise) he had always been ready to receive curious visitors at his home; lately he had taken to conducting them around the corner to the shed in which he kept the guillotine and—for a fee—operating it on bales of straw.[1] The enterprise was quite a success; "*force Anglais l'allaient voir*", and what indulgent papa would refuse his laughing daughters a chance to see the great blade of the guillotine come crashing down? The pink-and-white English misses sought the entertainment with gratifying frequency.

[1] See Desmazes, op. cit.

But it was not enough. Clément's finances remained insufficient for his needs. In what *lupanar*, in what *guinguette* did the solution first occur to him—to pawn the guillotine which had been entrusted to his personal care? The guillotine in pawn! Never had the mighty implement been reduced to so mean, so ignominious a condition.[1] And that it should be a Sanson who was responsible. . . .

The ignoble comedy did not stop there. Almost before Clément had had time to squander the cash, with tragic inevitability the *Procureur-général* ordered an execution. Anguishedly, the scapegrace headsman begged his creditor to release the machine for a day. He was refused. There was no escape. He was obliged to avow his dilemma to outraged authority, which, in turn, was obliged to redeem the pledge. Sternly, righteously, Clément was dismissed.

Shame, remorse, humiliation—if he felt any of these emotions—had no noticeable effect on him. The becoming thing to have done would have been to sink into a decline there and then, but, in reality, he did nothing of the sort. All this happened in 1847; Clément survived, unregenerate, until 1889—even, in his rakish course, repeating, as we have seen, the indecency of pawning the *bois de justice* and subsequently like an impoverished peer, transferring this family trophy to M. Tussaud.[2]

It was all very distressing—to the rest of us, if not to Clément

---

[1] The guillotine has always had its ups and downs. It was even "executed", so to speak, during the *Commune* "to consecrate the new liberty". The 137th Battalion of the 11th *arrondissement* (the quarter in which the guillotine was then lodged) smashed and burnt it before an enthusiastic crowd in April 1871. The immolation took place at the foot of a statue of Voltaire. See Maurice Garçon: *Histoire de la Justice sous la 111e République*, volume 1 (Librairie Arthème Fayard, Paris, 1957).

[2] The machine which he disposed of to M. Tussaud was clearly not the official machine then (1854) in use. This had been redeemed *and retained* by the authorities. M. Tussaud's acquisition was therefore presumably an item from the private museum at the rue des Marais and hence quite possibly what Clément said it was—the very guillotine used to execute the King. M. Dumas was assured by Henry Sanson that that historic implement was indeed in his possession.

himself—but one cannot altogether repress a certain sympathy with the skittish creature. Before his dismissal, urbanely philosophising with M. Rousseau during the latter's visit to his father, he mentioned that his daughter, contrary to convention, had married a Paris doctor. M. Rousseau manifested some surprise at the union of two such dissimiliar *milieux*. "Good heavens!" cried Clément reprovingly. "Try and look at things a bit more dispassionately. A surgeon is often compelled to sacrifice an unhealthy part in order to save a body. When the social body has a diseased member, isn't it reasonable to get rid of that, too?"

M. Rousseau brooded over the proposition for a moment or two. "I would like to observe", he said, "that there is a considerable difference between the two operations."

"Yes, Monsieur," replied Clément Sanson, "in the size of the knives."

The fellow had spirit.

CHAPTER THIRTEEN

BY a Decree issued on November 25th, 1870, the provincial executioners of France, already whittled down by successive ordinances from the pre-Revolutionary army of 160 to a mere handful, were finally abolished altogether. The functions so harmoniously shared and so capably performed by the Fereys, the Desmorets, the Etiennes, the Ganiers and the rest during several centuries at least were henceforward to be concentrated in the sole person of the Paris *bourreau*. He alone might decapitate his country's criminals, no matter in what remote district they were judged.

Who can doubt that this unique distinction—that of becoming the first "national" executioner—would have gone to Clément Sanson but for that sorry incident of the guillotine and the pawnbroker? He was only seventy-two when the new system was introduced (and still had eighteen years of life ahead of him) and in the ordinary course of events would doubtless have been actively employed. There is no prescribed retiring age for headsmen. How differently the Sansons might have ended. The last of their line, instead of besmirching his name, might have raised it to a yet greater eminence.

But while Clément Sanson was dicing his career away, a soberer *bourreau* was quietly perfecting his technique, effecting a suitable marriage, picking up useful little wrinkles from his father, and generally preparing himself for the honour which, in due course, was to be his instead of disgraced Clément's. This usurper was Louis Deibler, and, at the moment of Clément

Sanson's fall, he was assisting his father to remove heads at Rennes. He was the first man to graduate directly from assistant executioner to executioner for all France.

As the last of the families to produce chief executioners from father to son (the Desfourneaux, who began earlier and lasted longer in the trade, had been reduced to mere assistants and remained so until Henri Desfourneaux restored the family dignity in 1939) the Deiblers achieved a renown which almost rivals that of the Sansons. In the latter half of the nineteenth century and the first half of the twentieth, the very name was almost a synonym for "*bourreau*" and even today evokes the same horrific associations for Frenchmen as, say, Jack Ketch for the English.

Various external factors undoubtedly contributed to the Deiblers' rise to fame. Some really outstanding criminals came their way: Vacher, Landru, Caserio, Ravachol; and, although serious critics were not always impressed by their style, the development of the popular press resulted in their obtaining a degree of puffing denied to their predecessors. But these fortuitous circumstances do not lessen the family's merit in overcoming a major handicap: the Deiblers were not among the great pre-Revolutionary tribes and, indeed, were not even French.

The first of the brood to arrive in France was Joseph-Antoine, born at Altenberg (Bavaria) in 1789. His migration took place in either 1815 or 1816, and an authority on the clan [1] has suggested that he came as a soldier in the Bavarian forces of occupation. Like some of his compatriots similarly situated in a later epoch, he evidently preferred France over his own country and decided to settle—a fateful decision for some two thousand criminals in his adopted land.

Joseph Deibler began his new life unspectacularly as proprietor of a small wine-shop in the region of Lyon, but it was not a success—and perhaps that could have been foreseen in the

[1] See Jacques Delarue: *Les Deibler lyonnais* (*Reflets*, March 1954).

case of a German selling wine in France. Looking about for an occupation more suited to a stalwart young Bavarian, Joseph learned that Louis-Antoine-Stanislas Desmoret, headsman at Dijon, was in need of an assistant. He applied for the position, was interviewed, made a satisfactory impression, and was accepted. He could not have begun his career under a better instructor.

Joseph's entry into the profession of head-chopper is conventionally ascribed to a brutal Teutonic taste for the business —an instinctive *schadenfreude*—and there are dark tales of his childhood when the fetching little lad would give his elders no peace unless they took him on excursions to the Nuremberg Museum of Tortures to gloat in ecstatiated contemplation of wheels and thumbscrews, Iron Maidens, racks, blades and pincers.

It may all be quite true, of course. He may have been possessed of just such a natural disagreeableness of disposition; but there is an alternative—and better authenticated—explanation of his taking up the trade; for if his father, Fidelis, was a commonplace Bavarian farmer, his grandfather was the efficient and esteemed executioner of Biberach. Not only that: Deiblers (in a variety of orthographies) pullulate in the records of Germanic executing.[1] Clearly, that ingenious system of selection described by Maton de la Varenne did not invariably prevent the growth of family monopolies in the decapitation trade. Joseph was merely resuming a craft which was his by inheritance.

And for which he obviously had an inherited aptitude. No Desmoret would have tolerated an incompetent assistant for a

---

[1] C. Calvert refers to the Deublers "who are said to be connected with the Deibler family" and mentions that the Nuremberg records cite Albanus Friedrich Deubler as hangman of that city in the early nineteenth century. (See *A Hangman's Diary, Being the Journal of Master Franz Schmidt, Public Executioner of Nuremberg*, 1573-1617. Edited, with an Introduction, by Albrecht Keller, and translated by C. Calvert, B.A. (Lond.), and A. W. Gruner, M.A. (Oxon.), with an Introductory Essay by C. Calvert (Philip Allan & Co. Ltd., London, 1928).)

minute, and Joseph remained in his service for something like thirty years. The relationship in fact rapidly developed into a friendship as well as a purely professional connection, and when a son was born on February 13th, 1823, to Joseph and his wife (*née* Marguerite-Marie-Françoise Boyer), he was named after his father's employer: Louis-Antoine-Stanislas.

No novitiate in executing could have been more happily situated than Louis Deibler, with his conscientious parent and the great Desmorets always available to advise and counsel him. And moreover, in 1853, the Deiblers, for reasons not known, shifted to Algiers, where Joseph gave a helping hand to the local *bourreau*, Antoine-Joseph Rasseneux, and Louis was enabled to watch yet another master-craftsman at work.

As far as Louis was concerned, the Algiers phase was not solely of professional significance. M. Rasseneux's eighteen-year-old daughter, Zoé-Victorine, debarred by her father's *métier* from aspiring to marriage with ordinary young men, looked with a special interest on young Louis; he, in turn, similarly restricted in his choice of a helpmeet, was bound to be especially susceptible to Zoé's attractions. Antoine Rasseneux and Joseph Deibler, those benign executioners, watched the burgeoning of their offsprings' amours with sentimental tenderness. Within a matter of months, the union of the young couple was solemnised. A little later, Desmorets having gone to his reward and Joseph Deibler having been named chief executioner for the five departments of the west, all three returned to France and installed themselves at Rennes.

It has been said [1] that the aged Joseph was immoderately proud of his nomination as M. de Rennes and eager to see an heir born to the succession. Louis and Zoé did their best to oblige. In 1863, 1864, 1865 and 1867 respectively they produced four children: Anatole-Joseph, Berthe, Aglaé, and Ernest. Grandfather Joseph joyously declared the birth of the first of these to the local *mairie* himself. The succession assured, he

[1] See Paul Dornain: *De Sanson à Deibler* (Mignolet & Storz, Paris, 1934).

could now, in the sunset of life, afford to retire. Henceforward he could count on Louis to attend to local head-lopping and at the same time dream of the triumphs awaiting baby Anatole.

During eight years from the birth of his son, Louis Deibler carried out the duties which had been delegated to him. There were private woes to endure (his three other children all died before the age of five), but he did not allow them to interfere with the efficient discharge of his responsibilities to society. His record was so successful that when, in 1870, that Decree abolished the regional executioners, he was among those selected as worthy to be maintained in the capacity of assistant to the Parisian *bourreau*, M. Roch. In that rôle, he distinguished himself sufficiently to be chosen as M. Roch's replacement on the latter's death in 1879.

At first glance, his career looks like that of any able civil servant progressing from one deserved advancement to another. But was his reputation really justified? M. Dornain affirms [1] that "he had not got the assurance of the old man, nor his quick eye, nor his precision", while another writer [2]— and one who, unlike M. Dornain, had seen him in action— insisted that "he lacked prestige. With his clumsy bearing, his limping gait . . . he in no wise gave the impression of a head-chopper. If, instead of just operating a spring which worked the instrument for him, he had been obliged, as in the days of the old monarchy, to lift the axe or the two-handed sword and slice the victim's head off at one blow, he would have been incapable."

Most severe of all in his judgement of Louis Deibler was M. Grison,[3] a connoisseur if ever there was one, a fervent supporter of capital punishment and a man who liked to see it well done. Critically eyeing Deibler's executions, he found him "heavy, clumsy in his movements, indecisive," in

[1] See Dornain, op. cit.
[2] See Louis Hamon: *Police et Criminalité* (Flammarion, Paris, N.D.).
[3] See Grison, op. cit.

contrast to his predecessor, Nicolas Roch, "powerful and yet alert, quick". As an example of Deibler's displeasing technique, M. Grison noted that, instead of thrusting the victim abruptly against the *bascule* "with the apparent brutality of Roch", he would prolong the horror by placing his patient gently and cautiously on the fatal operating table.

This almost effeminate finickiness alternated with an unnecessary—an inaesthetic—callousness. Grison frankly admits that he was not himself an eye-witness of Louis Deibler's first "national" execution (four days after his nomination to office), but he clearly finds it easy to believe the story that the *bourreau* was obliged to bash his subject's head on the pavement in order to overcome the fellow's resistance. A *torero* taking a club to the bull would hardly be more outrageous.

Things were just as bad at a much later execution, that of the parricide Lantz. This time M. Grison was on the spot and personally vouches for the headsman's inadequacy. Deibler was "pale, agitated, nervous, trembling . . . less sure of himself than Lantz was" and actually went whining to the *commissaire* of police with a demand that the attendant journalists should be compelled to retire as they put him off his stroke. That was in 1882. Louis Deibler had had thirty or forty years in the game. Yet what a buffoon! He "took the victim by the shoulders, placed him on the *bascule* . . . settled and arranged him to his satisfaction, like a hairdresser settling his client in the chair". The foolery lasted more than a minute. "More than a minute!" exclaims Grison disdainfully. "In M. Roch's day it would scarcely have lasted ten to fifteen seconds!"

M. Grison, it must be repeated, was an austere critic of the old school. He had seen both Heindreicht and Roch at the height of their powers; it is likely that he somewhat resented the intrusion of these Boches and was predisposed to consider their performances mere casual butchery. At all events, he made no allowance for the difficulties with which Louis was contending. Louis Deibler, to quote M. Dornain once again, was endowed with "a sort of timidity which was not compensated for by the bitter disdain and bloody pride of his predecessor. . . . He was, moreover, better educated and had a greater understanding of the horror of his position." It was to his credit, surely, that with so much sensibility he was able to carry on at all.

Nor was his unease without justification. M. Grison might sneer as much as he liked at Louis' nervous temperament, but, not long after, the headsman's apprehensions were proved to have some genuine foundation—and, incidentally, received a considerable stimulus. It was the great epoch of the anarchists, those winningly ingenuous assassins, and embattled authority necessarily fought back through the *bourreau*. In July of 1892, Louis was instructed to proceed with the execution of the stupendous Ravachol, perhaps the most eminent of the brotherhood.

The friends of anarchy contemplated the imminent event with hot indignation. Reluctant—on principle, perhaps—to address themselves to the higher levels of government, they initiated a campaign of intimidation against the representative of established rule most directly concerned. A sequence of disquieting letters began to arrive at M. Deibler's neat apartment in the rue Vicq-d'Azir. Should Ravachol's head be lopped, the *bourreau* would be kidnapped, murdered, tortured with an ingenuity surpassing that of his most inventive forebears. Sensitive Deibler trembled responsively.

Letters addressed in the same menacing hand likewise arrived in the landlord's letter-box. Once executed, Ravachol should be revenged not only by the tormenting of the headsman but by the bombing of the headsman's house. Bombs at that time were exploding with almost comical frequency. There was nothing inherently improbable in the threat. The miserable Louis Deibler found himself not only shaking with a natural apprehension but also ejected from his home by the equally fearful proprietor. It even looked for a while as though

Ravachol's admirers would at least obtain a stay of execution since the timorous executioner was on the verge of refusing to perform.

Infirm of purpose . . . Mme Deibler, stern daughter of the Rasseneux, was not prepared to emulate Marie Ferey and herself work the guillotine in place of her husband, but her reproachful admonitions and then her angry insistence finally induced the backsliding *bourreau* to do his duty. The most ferocious anarchists were less terrifying in the long run than a disgruntled wife.

Ravachol was duly executed, none of the anarchists' horrendous threats were carried out, but the brotherhood still fancied that their warning letters to the headsman might prove effective in other cases. In 1894, the sinister envelopes were again delivered in connection with the proposed beheading of two more of the brethren. Once again Deibler unhappily fluttered; once again Mme Deibler triumphed in the battle for her husband's soul. Vaillant in February, Emile Henry in May lost their heads in accordance with the law and at the hands of Louis Deibler. When Caserio was sentenced to die for his really outstanding piece of anarchic propaganda—the assassination of President Carnot—the anarchists decided that stronger measures than simply despatching letters were needed to bring the *bourreau* to his senses.

A day or so after Henry's execution, Deibler was returning home from his customary evening promenade. He may or may not have noticed the newspaper-seller on the footpath. M. Dornain claims that the latter sang out "Votre *Dernière heure* est arrivée!" (the *Dernière heure* being a paper of the epoch) as the *bourreau* passed by and followed up this *jeu de mots* with a blow at Deibler's head. Two other individuals sprang forward, grabbed the executioner and carted him towards a vehicle stationed at the kerb. Deibler had actually been bundled inside before his anguished howls brought some passers-by to his aid.

He escaped whatever tweakings and twistings his assailants had planned, but the incident brought all his festering apprehensions to a head. The police instituted a series of round-ups in the quarter and provided a guard, but Deibler was not consoled. Some extramundane reassurance was needed, and from then on the *bourreau* was to be seen on pilgrimage to Lourdes (without any professional commitments to explain his presence) or (while in Paris) piously attending mass at his local church, Notre-Dame d'Auteuil. It was at this temple that the whispering congregation observed that the new communicant invariably approached the altar with gloved hands.

To this orthodox piety was added a still weirder spiritual sea-change. The unhappy Louis acquired what should be (but in fact, except rarely, is not) the executioner's occupational disease: hæmophobia, a morbid fear of blood. From the severed neck of Harsch (executed at Nancy in January 1897) the blood spurted more than two metres into the air and fell back on the *bourreau*. Stout old Joseph would hardly have bothered to wipe the stuff away, but his pernickety son was positively shaken, never indeed recovered. At the execution of Carrara, the mushroom murderer, in the following year, Louis, even though the job was as clean as a whistle, suddenly collapsed, hysterically bellowing that he was drenched in blood. One doesn't like to think what M. Grison would have said.

The neurosis burgeoned alarmingly. Within his home, it is said, Louis wandered about like a Lady Macbeth, begging his family for reassurance that his hands, which he was forever mechanically dry-washing, were free of the fluid by which he lived. His nights were filled with frightful nightmares in which he saw the guillotine, infinitely duplicated, stretching away to the horizon of his subconscious. In December of 1898, having participated in the removal of more than one thousand human heads, the hag-ridden executioner abdicated in favour of his son, Anatole.

Anatole Deibler would have been able to plead every justification had he shown a timidity and melancholia even exceed-
ing that of his father. As a child, his schoolfellows had only
concealed their pharisaic aversion when they needed Anatole
to play the part of headsman in their pretty childish games of
cops-and-robbers. Later on, when, as we have seen, he waived
his *de facto* privilege of exemption from military service, the
rest of the regiment either mocked him or shrank from him.
When he obtained employment in a department store, he
encountered the same treatment. And when, resignedly, he
consented to replace his father as M. de Paris—what tantrums he
provoked, what regrettable displays of peevishness. Old Louis'
aides included members of such noble executing families as the
Desfourneaux, the Etiennes, the Bergers and the Desmorets.
Each of them considered he had a better right to the office than
a man whose father had repeatedly let the profession down
and who himself had tried to flee his responsibilities as though
they were somehow shameful. M. Dornain hints that, in their
chagrin, the assistants even tried to sabotage the guillotine itself.

None of these circumstances—nor the spectacle of what it
had cost his parent to serve as executioner—broke Anatole's
morale. Writing in 1882, when the young man was still
counter-jumping, M. Grison prophesied that it would not be
long before he joined papa, and, in fact, it was only a few
weeks later that he first took his stand by the guillotine in the
capacity of assistant. On December 31st, 1898, although Louis
was still nominally in charge of operations, it was Anatole
who in reality attended to the beheading of that remarkable
sadist, Joseph Vacher. That confused head was trimmed from
its trunk with neatness and despatch and, in the following
month, Anatole was officially designated M. de Paris. After a
few preliminary try-outs in the provinces, he made his bow
in Paris before a select audience which included the former
British Prime Minister, Lord Rosebery.[1]

[1] See *Les Annales politiques et littéraires*, February 12th, 1899.

His subject was the nineteen-year-old Alfred Peugnez, and the press saluted the new *bourreau's* prowess with enthusiasm. "All the newspapers agree in paying tribute to young M. Deibler, whose Parisian début revealed a handiness and an ease worthy of an old practitioner. Youthful, elegant, dressed in a frock-coat of sombre hue like a second at some *exclusive* duel, he typifies to perfection the modern *bourreau*. After this happy beginning, one can safely predict for him a fine career and a respectable number of performances." [1]

Astute forecast! The career which began with Vacher took in such notables as Landru, Gorguloff and the "chauffeurs de la Drôme", and the number of performances eventually reached the undeniably respectable figure of three hundred and forty.

Names and numbers mean nothing by themselves. The main thing was that Anatole declined to go in for the vapours as his father had done, and invariably demonstrated a smooth and adroit technique and a fitting gravity of demeanour. Bearded, irreproachably garbed, sure of himself, there was never any question of pounding his patients' heads on the ground or collapsing from hæmophobiac attacks. His mien was that of an Academician preoccupied with some ponderous lexicographical problem.

Only once was his massive urbanity shaken, and on that occasion not even M. Grison could have blamed him. In March 1918, he and his tools were lent to the Belgian government (in fact, although not in law, Belgium had dispensed with capital punishment for more than fifty years past) so that, exceptionally, an example might be made of Camille Verfeuille, a Belgian soldier condemned for the murder of a servant-girl.[2]

The night of Deibler's arrival at Adinkerque had been selected by the Germans for an especially ferocious bombardment; he and his aides were compelled to pass several hours in an underground shelter. The same indiscriminate slaughter—

[1] Ibid.   [2] See Dornain, op. cit.

so different from the decent selectivity of the guillotine—was
going on at Furnes when they reached that town to proceed
with the execution. The *bourreau* and his assistants were appalled. To operate, as intended, on the market-place was out
of the question: the walls of the prison at least gave the illusion
of security, and it was within these walls that Verfeuille was
hurriedly and nervously decapitated. The headsmen were on
their way back to Paris within the hour, shaken and resentful.
"What's the idea," protested one of them, "sending us into
the middle of a battlefield?" They were peaceful creatures and
accustomed to only one sort of sudden death.

M. Deibler rapidly recovered his serenity. He had his troubles
like other men, and, like other men, survived them. Heurte-
loup, the carpenter who built the guillotines, considered himself a cut above the man who operated them and refused his
daughter's hand to the lovelorn *bourreau*. Subsequently he
married Rosalie Rogis (her sister, Juliette, was the mother of
André Obrecht; her niece, Georgette, married Henri Desfourneaux; her brother, Louis, became an assistant to Anatole—
a talented family), but their son, Roger-Isidore, died at an
early age. There was a considerable family upset when their
daughter, Marcelle, fell in love with her cousin André and her
mother forbade her to do what she herself had done and marry
a headsman.[1]

No doubt these domestic dramas were painful, but in a way
they add the final touches to the transmogrification of the
executioner; for, with Anatole Deibler, that officer ceased to
be a nightmarish and paralysing spook and became the respectable bourgeois. Anatole was an accomplished cyclist and a
popular member of the Auteuil Bicycling Club; at the Café
de Marseille in the avenue de Versailles, he and Louis Rogis
made a formidable partnership at billiards; with another of
his aides, Léopold Desfourneaux, he was a shrewd player of
bélote; he enjoyed his week-end drives in the country, an

[1] See Dornain, op. cit.

hour's meditative fishing. It was Anatole Deibler whose irreproachable existence, modesty of demeanour and conscientious craftsmanship made it possible for Louis Rogis to boast that "before the war, we had to cover up our identities in order to get a spare-time situation. These days my name is in the telephone directory. . . ."[1]

In February of 1939, Anatole Deibler collapsed with a fatal heart attack in the *Métro* station while setting off to execute Pilorges in the provinces. Curiously enough, he was bound for Rennes, where Grandfather Joseph might be said to have started the family's whole destiny.

[1] Ibid.

CHAPTER FOURTEEN

How has society compensated, or sought to compensate, the *bourreaux* for the ostracism, the frustrated loves, the nightmares—not to mention the inconvenient working hours —which have so often been inseparable from their office? The reward has varied greatly. At one extreme, the convict-executioners of the Guiana penal settlements might legitimately complain of official parsimony. For slicing off a fellow-prisoner's head, they received a tin of sardines, two bottles of red wine and ten francs [1]—sheer sweating.

At the other extreme, the annoyances inherent in the trade were, frankly, made worth any man's while. When, in 1688, Charles Sanson was promoted to Paris, *le Roi soleil* laid down his servant's emoluments on a princely scale: [2]

"Louis, by the grace of God King of France and Navarre, to all those who shall see these presents, greetings! By order of our Court of the Parliament of Paris, the eleventh August of the present year, it having been ordained for the reasons hereinafter set out that Charles Sanson known as Longval shall alone fulfil the office of Executioner of High Justice in our city, provostry and viscounty of Paris subject to his obtaining our letters patent for the said office; wherefore be it known that in view of the good account given us of the said Charles Sanson known as Longval, we have, in accordance with the said order, given and granted and do by these presents give and grant to him the status of Executioner of the High Works

[1] See Le Boucher, op. cit.   [2] See Lenotre, op. cit.

(134)

and Criminal Sentences in our aforesaid city, provostry and viscounty of Paris, heretofore held and exercised by Nicolas Levasseur, known as La Rivière, last incumbent thereof, the same having been discharged by the said order of our said Court of the Parliament of Paris, and added, under the counter-seal of our Chancery, in respect of the said office and its tenure, future exercise, enjoyment and use by the aforesaid Sanson, to the rights of levy in the fairs and markets of our said city, provostry and viscounty of Paris, products, gains, revenues and emoluments, such and similar as have well and properly been enjoyed by the incumbents of like offices; to wit: enjoyment of the house and habitation of the Pillory of *les Halles*, its appurtenances and dependencies, without let or hindrance for whatsoever cause, and furthermore the right to exact from each merchant bearing eggs on his back or by hand one egg, from each saddle-load two eggs, from each cart-load a *demi-quarteron*, and from each basket of apples, pears, grapes and other produce whether arriving by land or by water in boats carrying the same load as a horse one *sou*; for each laden horse the same amount and for each cart two *sous*; for those bringing, whether by land or water, green peas, medlars, hemp-seed, mustard-seed, poulavin, millet, walnuts, chestnuts, hazel-nuts his spoonful as has always been the custom; from each itinerant merchant bringing on his back or by hand butter, cheese, poultry and fresh-water fish, six *deniers*; for each horse, one *sou*; for each cartload of beans, two *sous*; for each tip-cart twenty *sous* and a carp; and for each bag of peas or broad beans in pods one *sou*, and for each basket six *deniers*; and for each case of oranges and lemons brought in by itinerant merchants either by water or by land, one *sou*; for each waggon-load of oysters in the shell one *quarteron* and for each boat-load in proportion and for every person bringing brooms, one broom; for every horse-load, two; and for every cart-load, six; for every merchant bringing in coal, his potful; from the sworn rope-makers, rope for the executions; all of which rights have always been levied both in our own city of Paris and in other parts of our Kingdom, which the said Sanson will enjoy as also exemption from all levies in respect of night-watch, guards, bridges, ferries, receipt of wine and other beverages for his own provender, with the right to carry arms both offensive and defensive, himself and his servants, on account of his office."

This pretty custom was known as the right of "*havage*", and Lenotre estimates its value to the Paris executioner at 60,000 *livres* a year in the late eighteenth century in addition to the prescribed salary of 6,000 *livres* per annum. Sixty-six thousand livres! [1] Even though popular disesteem forbade the headsman to touch the merchandise with his dishonoured hands, obliging him to serve himself with a long metal spoon, a sum like that made up for a lot of such prissy superciliousness.

In the provinces, the executioners' salaries were markedly less lavish and sometimes the poor devils were dependent entirely on payment by results. At Rennes, for example, piecework was paid for at the following cheese-paring rates: sixty *livres* for breaking a man on the wheel, thirty for hanging him, ten for whipping or branding him: and even the least of these corrections was ordered with discouraging infrequency. [2]

To live in any sort of style at all, then, the regional *bourreaux* were dependent on the *havage*, and when, in 1775, this lien was withdrawn as far as all farinaceous stuffs were concerned, the economic circumstances of those functionaries were catastrophically affected. By way of compensation for the loss, some of them were granted alternative privileges of a peculiar and insufficient nature—the right to operate primitive gambling-places or, at Arras, to collect and sell whatever dead horses might be available in the district [3]—but it was a feeble recompense. The headsman of France, like so many of their

[1] Approximately £2,640.
[2] See Le Bour'his-Kerbiziet, op. cit.
[3] See Lenotre, op. cit.

compatriots at about that time, were suddenly made aware of a changing order of things.

They had not long to wait before the change became absolute. The revolutionaries, for all that they called on the *bourreaux'* services with a gusto unimagined by the dethroned tyrant, were nonetheless prepared to sacrifice even those indispensable collaborators to doctrinaire enthusiasm. So feudal a relic as *havage* in any form was inadmissible and was duly decreed out of existence. The headsmen, bucking against the inevitable, wailed in chorus: Jean-Louis Desmorets wrote frantically from Laon demanding that the Ministry of Justice bear in mind his thirty-six years of loyal and unimpeachable service: from Arras, Pierre Outredebanque, seeing those dead horses vanish overnight, clamoured for a pension; not an executioner in France but felt himself, and rightly, to have been swindled.[1]

At the beginning of 1791, Charles-Henri Sanson, sadly naïve, attempted to whip up a little official sympathy for his position. The new regulation, he made clear, simply did not allow him to cope with his obligations, let alone live in a manner consonant with his high position. Let the authorities consider his expenses. Six hundred *livres* each to his two brothers for dealing with administrative correspondence while he was busy head-chopping; a total of 1,200 for his servants, another 300 for his three drivers; 1,200 to his old mother in accordance with the provision allotted by law under the old régime; without mentioning harness for the horses, food for his household of sixteen, the care and replacement of his tools. At a minimum estimate he needed the better part of 30,000 livres—and that made no allowance for occasional entertainments or savings against an outcast old age.[2]

Well accustomed, no doubt, to bureaucratic immobility, the *bourreau* patiently waited a full eight months before pressing for an answer—months during which work had to go on

[1] Ibid.   [2] Ibid.

as usual and when, as it happened, staff problems were more
than ordinarily tiresome: the pace at which tribunals were
condemning felons to death obliged him to have his team of
helpers in a permanent state of readiness, and, he pointed out
querulously, "since I can't be everywhere at once myself, I
need people on whom I can rely. The public, after all, still
wants things done decently. The sort of people required for
this work want twice the wages paid in previous years. Only
last Saturday they came to tell me that they wouldn't be able
to go on unless I could give them a rise of one-quarter at
least. . . ."[1]

But not even the threat of a strike was enough to hurry the
administration along. Only on June 13th, 1793—perhaps in a
flush of enthusiasm for executions and executioners arising
from the introduction of the guillotine—was it decreed that
M. de Paris should henceforward receive an annual stipend of
10,000 *livres*.[2] Provincial *bourreaux* operating in towns with a
population between 100,000 and 300,000 drew 6,000 *livres*,
between 50,000 and 100,000 the fee dropped to 4,000 *livres*;
the headsman with less than 50,000 heads to choose from made
a pittance of 2,400. A little later[3], the authorities grudgingly
allocated an additional 36 *livres* travelling allowance (when
applicable) and agreed that transport of the guillotine should
no longer be a personal charge on the executioner.

What a contrast with things as they were only a few years
before, when Maurice Le Glaouër could submit a bill [4] of just
under 140 *livres* for a single execution at Brest (with a population well under 10,000) and know that it would be paid
promptly and in full. And how reasonable his charges were
when one looks into them: 21 *livres* for hacking off the condemned man's hand, 30 for providing the gibbet (the fellow
was to be hanged as well as mutilated), 4 for the use of a cleaver

---

[1] See Lenotre, op. cit.
[2] Approximately £400.
[3] Décret du 3 frimaire, an II (November 23rd, 1793).
[4] See Le Bour'his-Kerbiziet, op. cit.

to sever the wrist, 6 for taking the victim down from the gibbet and shoving him in a coffin, 75 for his own and his assistant's travelling expenses. . . . Seventeen executions a year at charges which the meanest clerk could not quibble over were enough to earn Maurice the sum which his son, Hervé, was now paid for carrying out heaven knew how many jobs.

M. Le Bour'his-Kerbiziet notes that Hervé Le Glaouër, in spite of the government's retrenchment policy towards executioners, was able to rake up a substantial sum for the purchase of a house at Quimper, and goes on to suggest that there were probably worthwhile pickings for an alert heads- man. One would like to think so, and such may have been the case in Brittany. Elsewhere in France, however, the niggardly new law literally drove many of the country's best *bourreaux* out of business. Resignations became so numerous that, during the Terror, the Public Accusers of one department were for ever pestering their opposite numbers in another to lend them a *bourreau* for a few days to clear up the accumulated criminals.[1] For the sake of a few *livres*, the Revolutionaries destroyed the flower of the old executing families.

Later governments were even less generous in their treat- ment of the headsman. In 1832, the Paris incumbent was receiving the shamefully small sum of 8,000 francs [2] for his services, and his provincial colleagues were paid salaries which dwindled from 5,000 francs for Lyon to 4,000 for Bordeaux and Rouen, and so down to 2,000 for towns with a population of less than 20,000.[3] In 1849, M. de Paris had 3,000 francs lopped off his salary,[4] and in the following year the remainder was, so to say, guillotined of another 1,000.[5] By this time, the doyen of the provincial executioners, M. de Lyon, was down

[1] See Lenotre, op. cit.
[2] Approximately £320. A franc was almost exactly equivalent to a *livre*.
[3] Ordonnance du roi du 7 octobre, 1832.
[4] Arrêté du 9 mars, 1849.
[5] Décret du 26 juin, 1850.

to 3,000 francs, MM. de Bordeaux, de Rouen and de Toulouse to 2,400 each, and the rest just 2,000.

The Decree of November 25th, 1870, restored 2,000 francs to the Paris *bourreau's* salary, raising it once again to 6,000, payable monthly. But what a mockery was this apparent remorse on the part of the authorities! By the same edict they landed the then holder of the office, M. Roch, with immeasurably more work than they were entitled to exact for so feeble a rise; for M. de Paris was henceforward M. de France, personally responsible for every head-chopping required throughout the Republic.

As to the provincial men—the backbone of the profession, after all—they were dismissed with the *dégagé* brutality of which only governments are capable: "As from January 1st, 1871, the chief executioners and their assistants in service within the continental territory of France will be relieved of their individual posts. Each of them will cease to draw his salary one month after receipt of such notification at his home to be delivered by the Prefect of the Department. . . ."

A few of them were saved from total penury by being retained among M. Roch's two First Class Assistants (on 4,000 francs per year) or three Second Class Assistants (on 3,000 francs per year).

None of the profession could have been satisfied with the arrangement, and it must have been small consolation that the decree guaranteed them free travel (when on official business) by the fastest trains and eight francs per day travelling allowance. Eight francs! The *Roi soleil* would have died sooner than treat his servants with such sordid avarice.

And even the eight francs were far from secure. Towards the end of the nineteenth century and at the beginning of the twentieth, France was undergoing a spasm of humanitarianism which would have delighted Dr Guillotin himself. President Grévy to begin with, then President Loubet, then President Fallières systematically commuted such capital sentences as were pronounced, but a few unavoidably sneaked through. From time to time, some sunnily confident murderer would have the unpleasant surprise of being wrenched from his cell and laid on the *bascule*.

These occasional executions were too much altogether for the buoyant philanthropists of the day. Since they could not achieve formal abolition of the death penalty, they looked about for other means of doing their fellow-men a good turn and, unable to help the murderers, decided to hurt the heads-man. The benign socialist Jaurès (who might have felt differently if he had known that he himself was destined for assassination) devised a beautifully simple and effective scheme. On July 5th, 1906, the budgetary committee suppressed all the *bourreau's* allowances.[1]

It was distinctly unkind. Anatole Deibler was thus committed to meet out of his own pocket not only the expenses of his journeyings from one place to another but also the cost of the upkeep of the guillotine. Only a deep devotion to his art and a pious respect for the machine which he had inherited from his father could have induced him to bear with the affront and remain in office.

Fortunately the situation did not last long and Deibler's travels during the period were negligible. Presidential clemency was still forthcoming as regularly as clockwork, but the beneficiaries were unable to accept their good fortune with a suitable grace. Pronouncement of the death sentence almost provoked a grin from the man in the dock, and when one especially outrageous bandit not only forbore to request the President's mercy but actually asked him to provide a girl-friend to cheer up the condemned cell, the indignant deputies re-established the headsman's allowances on the spot.[2]

But there was no question of restoring the *bourreau's* ancient prosperity. M. Deibler was conscientious and hardworking— in one particularly good year he removed heads at the rate of

---

[1] See Dornain, op. cit.   [2] Ibid.

nearly one a fortnight—but his pay remained until the day of his death at 10,000 francs [1]—and with post-war inflation that was not a lot.

Even so, he was better off than today's executioner with a monthly income of 60,000; and as for today's assistants. . . . On a salary roughly equal to £14 per month—and no pension to look forward to—is it any wonder that they are obliged to take on outside employment in addition to their proper jobs? That both of them use blades in the course of their secondary professions—one is a hairdresser, the other a butcher—helps not at all. Good executing requires single-mindedness and application, and from today's assistants must come (there is no heir-apparent) tomorrow's chief executioners. It would be sad for all concerned if M. Obrecht's successor were ever, from mere lack of professional pride, to echo the reply which Sanson made from commendable sensibility when asked his feelings during an execution.

"Monsieur," he said, "I am always in a great hurry to get it over."

---

[1] Arrêté ministériel du 24 janvier, 1923.

INDEX

Cook, Thomas, 74
Corday, Charlotte, 81
Crébillon, Claude-Prosper Jolyot de 34
Croker, John Wilson, 13, 61
Crozes, Abbé Abraham-Sébastien, 63, 80
Cullerier, Dr Michel, 44–8

Dabat, B. & P., 76
Damiens, Robert-François, 7
Danjou, Henri, 76, 106
Danton, Georges-Jacques, 61, 100
Dauban, C. A., 66
David, Louis, 8
Davies, Pamela, xi
Decaisne, Dr E., 84, 86
Decaisne, Dr G., 84
Deibler, Aglaé, 124
Deibler, Anatole-Joseph-Francis, 95, 104, 108, 124, 125, 129–33, 141
Deibler, Anatole-Joseph-Francis (Mme) (see Rogis, Rosalie)
Deibler, Berthe, 124
Deibler, Ernest, 124
Deibler, Fidelis, 123
Deibler, Joseph-Antoine, 103, 122–4, 133
Deibler, Louis-Antoine-Stanislas, 53, 63, 92, 98, 121, 122, 124–30
Deibler, Louis-Antoine-Stanislas (Mme) (see Rasseneux, Zoé-Victorine)
Deibler, Marcelle, 132
Deibler, Roger-Isidore, 132
Delarue, Jacques, xi, 3, 122
Descartes, René, 5
Desfourneaux, Edouard, 101
Desfourneaux, Jules-Henri, 75, 100, 101, 108, 122, 132
Desfourneaux, Léopold, 132
Desfourneaux, René-Henri, 130
Desgenettes, René, 37, 51
Desmaze, Charles, 84, 93, 118
Desmorets, Charles-Constant, 118
Desmorets, Citizen, 99
Desmorets, François, 101
Desmorets, Jean-Louis, 137
Desmorets, Louis-Antoine-Stanislas, 123, 124

Desmorets, Simon, 102
Desmoulins, Camille, 3
D'Espezel, Pierre, xi, 33, 45
Deubler, Albanus Friedrich, 123
Dickens, Charles, 3, 4
Diderot, Denis, 8, 34
Dornain, Paul, 124–6, 128, 130–3
Dubarry (Mme) (see Barry)
Dubois, M., 53
Dubut, Jeanne-Renée, 111
Dubut, Marthe, 111, 112
Du Camp, Maxime, 19, 71
Ducrest, Georgette, 17
Du Deffand, Mme, 74
Dumas, Alexandre (père), 116–19
Duport-Dutertre, Marguerite-Louis-François, 16, 30–2, 34
Dürer, Albrecht, 25
Dutton, Geoffrey (Mr & Mrs), xi

Edward III, 21
Eiffel, Alexandre-Gustave, 74
Elliott, Grace Dalrymple, 114
Evrard, Dr Alfred, 84

Fallières, President, 95, 140
Fère, Guyot de (G.D.F.), 2, 61
Ferey, Marie, 107, 128
Fleischmann, Hector, 13, 39–41, 43, 45, 46, 52, 61, 68, 70, 99, 107
Fluraut, 34
Fortin, Captain, 64
Fouquier-Tinville, Antoine-Quentin, 1, 97
Fournier, Dr, 89
François le Gros, 81
Froidcourt, Georges de, 25, 55

Ganier, Charles-Alexandre, 101
Ganier, Félix, 108
Ganier, Henri, 101
Ganier, Jacques, 96, 98, 101
Ganier, Jacques-Joseph, 107
Garçon, Maurice, 119
Gastellier, René-Georges, 83
Gautier, Pierre, 80
Giraud, Pierre, 56, 58, 60
Giraud, Robert, 3
Giraudoux, Jean, 117